22 DAYS IN SPAIN AND PORTUGAL

THE ITINERARY PLANNER

RICK STEVES

John Muir Publications
Santa Fe, New Mexico

Other JMP travel guidebooks by Rick Steves
Europe Through the Back Door
Europe 101: History, Art and Culture for the Traveler (with
   Gene Openshaw)
Mona Winks: Self-Guided Tours of Europe's Top Museums
   (with Gene Openshaw)
22 Days in Europe
22 Days in Great Britain
22 Days in Germany, Switzerland and Austria
22 Days in Norway, Sweden and Denmark
22 Days in France

Thanks to Dave Hoerlein, Mike McGregor and Gene Openshaw for research
assistance.

John Muir Publications, P.O. Box 613, Santa Fe, NM 87504
© 1986, 1987, 1989 by Rick Steves
Cover and maps © 1986, 1987, 1989 by John Muir Publications
All rights reserved. Published 1989
Printed in the United States of America
Third edition. Second printing.

Library of Congress Cataloging-in-Publication Data
Steves, Rick, 1955-
   22 days in Spain and Portugal: the itinerary planner/Rick
Steves.—3rd ed.
      p. cm.
   Rev. ed. of: Spain and Portugal in 22 days. 1986.
   ISBN 0-945465-06-8
   1. Spain—Description and travel—1981- —Guide-books.
2. Portugal—Description and travel—1981- —Guide-books.
I. Steves, Rick, 1955– Spain and Portugal in 22 days. II. Title.
III. Title: Twenty-two days in Spain and Portugal.
DP14.S76 1989
914.6'0483—dc19   89-3035
                                                           CIP

22 Days Series Editor   Richard Harris
Design/Production   Mary Shapiro
Maps   Jim Wood and David C. Hoerlein
Cover Map   Jennifer Dewey
Typography   Copygraphics, Inc.

Distributed to the book trade by:
W.W. Norton & Company, Inc.
New York, New York

CONTENTS

Spain & Portugal

HOW TO USE THIS BOOK

The Iberian peninsula is a fiesta of traditional folk life, memorable new taste treats, great buildings where the glorious winds of the past can still be heard, world-class art treasures, and friendly people. With Spain's current economic and cultural boom, the approaching Olympics in 1992, the 500th anniversary of Columbus's voyage, and an upcoming World's Fair, this is a particularly exciting time to visit the area. It's a cheap place to travel, and as you study, you'll see how many thrilling sights Spain and Portugal pack into this sunny peninsula.

This book sorts through all the "must see" sights, organizing the region into a carefully thought out, thoroughly tested step-by-step itinerary. It gives you the best basic 22 days in Spain and Portugal and a suggested way to use each of those days most efficiently. *22 Days in Spain and Portugal* is your problem-solver, your friendly fisherman, your Spaniard in a jam. It's your handbook for the best independent budget 22-day Iberian adventure.

Realistically, most travelers are interested in the predictable biggies—Alhambra, Prado, and flamenco. This tour covers them while mixing in a good dose of "back door" intimacy: sun-parched Andalusian hill towns, forgotten Algarve fishing villages, and desolate La Mancha windmills.

While the trip is designed as a car tour, it also makes a great three-week train/bus trip. Each day's journey is adapted for train and bus travel with explanations, options, and appropriate schedule information included.

The trip starts and ends in Madrid, but you may consider flying into Lisbon and out of Madrid (or vice versa). This "open-jaws" flight plan saves lots of driving time and costs no more than flying in and out of the same city. Get specifics from your travel agent. To make an open-jaws itinerary fit this 22-day plan, you'd probably skip a few cities in the north and visit others as side trips from Madrid and Lisbon.

Either a three-week car rental split two ways or a three-week first class Eurailpass costs about $400. Flying round-trip to Madrid costs $600 to $800. For room and board, figure $25 a day for 22 days, totaling $550. This is a feasible budget, if you know the tricks. (If you don't, see my book *Europe Through the Back Door*.) Add $200 or $300 fun money and you've got yourself a great Iberian holiday for under $2,000. Do it!

This book should be read through completely before your trip and then used as a rack to hang more ideas on. As you study and travel and plan and talk to people, you'll fill it with notes. It's your tool.

The book is flexible. It's completely modular and adaptable to an Iberian trip of any length. You'll find 22 days, each built with the same sections:

1. **Introductory overview** of the day.
2. Hour-by-hour **Suggested Schedule** that I recommend for each day.
3. List of the most important **Sightseeing Highlights** (rated: ▲▲▲ Don't miss; ▲▲ Try hard to see; ▲ Worthwhile if you can make it).
4. **Transportation** plan for drivers, plus an adapted plan with schedules for train and bus travelers.
5. **Food** and **Accommodations**: How and where to find the best budget places, including addresses, phone numbers, and my favorites.
6. **Helpful Hints** on orientation, shopping, transportation, and day-to-day chores.
7. An easy-to-read **map** locating recommended places.
8. **Itinerary Options** for those with more or less than the suggested time, or with particular interests.

At the back of the book, I've included posttour options for those with more time. There are also thumbnail sketches of Spanish and Portuguese culture, history, art, food, and language as well as lists of festivals, foreign phrases, and other helpful information.

Efficient Travelers Think Ahead

"Ad libbing" a holiday through Spain and Portugal sounds fine, but those with limited time and money can't afford the serious mistakes that plague careless travelers. An itinerary enables you to hit the festivals, bullfights, and museums on the right day. Travelers who plan ahead experience more, save time, and spend less money.

This itinerary assumes you are a well-organized traveler who lays departure groundwork on arrival. Read the entire book before you leave, and then read each suggested schedule a day ahead. Keep a list of all the things that should be taken care of and ward off problems whenever possible before they happen. Try to travel outside of peak season—July and August—so finding hotels won't be a problem; use local tourist information centers; and don't be an "ugly American." If you expect to travel smart, you will. If you insist on being confused, your trip will be a mess.

General Warning: Tourists are prime targets of thieves throughout Spain and Portugal. While hotel rooms are generally safe and muggings are very rare, cars are commonly broken into, purses are snatched, and pockets are picked. Be on guard, wear a money belt, leave nothing of value in your car, and park carefully.

When to Go

Spring and fall offer the best combination of good weather, light crowds, long days, and plenty of tourist and cultural activities. Summer and winter travel have their pros and predictable cons. July and August is most crowded in coastal areas and uncomfortably hot and dusty in the interior. For weather specifics, see the climate chart. Whenever you anticipate crowds, try to arrive early and call hotels in advance. Call from one hotel to the next; your receptionist can help you.

Prices

There are about 120 Spanish *pesetas* (ptas) in a U.S. dollar and 150 Portuguese *escudos* (they use the $ sign after the number, e.g., 150$ = US $1) in a U.S. dollar. For simplicity, I've priced many things in this book in dollar approximations. My listings are for travelers with daily room-and-board budgets ranging from $15 to $50. Hotels are listed in these general price categories for double rooms with breakfast and, except for cheap listings, usually with private shower. (Singles generally cost one-third less than doubles. Triples and quads are plentiful and cheaper per person. Off-season prices are a few dollars less.)

	Cheap	Inexpensive	Moderate	Expensive
Spain	under $17 (up to 2,000 pesetas)	$17 to 30 (2,000-3,500 pesetas)	$30 to 50 (3,500-6,000 pesetas)	$50 to 100 (over 6,000 pesetas)
Portugal	under $14 (up to 2,000 escudos)	$14 to 23 (2,000-3,500 escudos)	$23 to 40 (3,500-6,000 escudos)	$40 to 80 (over 6,000 escudos)

In this book, the words "cheap," "inexpensive," "moderate," and "expensive" will be used only to show these relative categories. These prices, as well as the hours, telephone numbers, and so on, are always changing, and I have tossed timidity out the window knowing you'll understand that this book, like any guidebook, starts growing old before it's even printed. Please don't expect Spain and Portugal to have stood entirely still since this book was written, and do what you can to call ahead or double-check hours and prices when you arrive.

Scheduling

Your overall itinerary strategy is a fun challenge. Read through this book and note the problem days: Mondays, when many museums are closed, and Sundays, when public transportation is meager. Saturdays are virtually weekdays. It's good to mix intense and relaxed periods. Every trip needs at least a few slack days. Things like banking, laundry stops, mail days, and picnics should be anticipated and planned for. While this itinerary works (I get piles of "having-a-great-trip" postcards from traveling readers), some find the pace hectic. My goal has been maximum thrills at a reasonable tempo. Skip places or add days according to your travel style.

Train travelers should realize that "the trains in Spain are sometimes a pain," making the full 22-day itinerary impractical by rail. Train travelers will want to streamline with overnight train rides and skip a few out-of-the-way places as recommended in the text.

Accommodations

Spain and Portugal offer about the cheapest rooms in Europe. Most accommodations are government-regulated with posted prices. Throughout Iberia, you'll find a good selection. Generally—except for the most touristy places—reservations are not necessary. July and August are most crowded.

While prices are low, street noise is high. Always ask to see your room first. You can check the price posted on the door, consider potential night noise problems, ask for another room, and even bargain the price down. Breakfast and showers can cost extra, and meals may or may not be required. In most towns, the best places to look for rooms are in the old—and most interesting—quarter, near the main church and near the station.

Both Spain and Portugal have plenty of youth hostels and campgrounds, but I don't recommend them. Youth hostels are often a headache, campgrounds hot and dusty, and the savings, considering the great bargains on other accommodations, are not worth the trouble. Hotels, pensions, and so forth are easy to find, inexpensive, and, when chosen properly, an important part of experiencing the Spanish and Portuguese cultures. If you're on a starvation budget or just want to camp or hostel, there is plenty of information available through the National Tourist Office and in appropriate guidebooks.

Each country has its handy categories of accommodations. Make a point to learn them.

In Spain, government-regulated places have blue-and-white plaques outside their doors clearly marked F, CH, P, HsR, Hs, or H. These are the various categories in ascending order of price and comfort:

Fonda (F) is your basic inn, often with a small bar serving cheap meals.

Casas de Huéspedes (CH) are guest houses without bars. Pensiones (P) are like CHs but serve meals. Hostales (Hs) have nothing to do with youth hostels. They are quite comfortable, are rated from one to three stars, and charge $15 to $30 for a double. Hotels (H) are rated with one to five stars and go right up to world-class luxury places. Hostal-Residencia (HsR) and Hotel-Residencia (HR) are the same as Hs and H class with no meals except breakfast.

Any regulated place will have a *libro de reclamaciones* (complaint book). A request for this book will generally solve any problem you have in a jiffy.

Portugal's system starts at the bottom with Residencias, Albergarias, and Pensões (one to four stars). These pensions are cheap ($10 to $30 doubles) and often tasteful, traditional, comfy, and family-run. Hotels (one to five stars) are more expensive ($15 to $60 doubles).

While these rating systems are handy, they are not perfect. You may find a CH that is cheaper and nicer than an Hs.

Both Spain and Portugal have local bed-and-breakfast-type accommodations, usually in touristy areas where locals decide to open up a spare room and make a little money on the side. These are called *camas, habitaciones,* or *casas particulares* in Spain and *quartos* in Portugal. They are very cheap, always interesting, and usually a good experience.

Spain and Portugal also have luxurious government-sponsored historic inns. These *paradores* (Spain) and *pousadas* (Portugal) are often renovated castles, palaces, and monasteries, many with great views and incredible atmosphere. Always a great value, their prices range from $35 to $100 per double. Pousadas have a reputation for serving fine food, while paradores are often disappointing in this respect. The paradores of central and northern Spain are usually better than Mediterranean ones. Reservations are a good idea any time and are virtually required in the summer. The receptionists usually speak English and are happy to call the next one to make a reservation for you.

There is plenty of information on these places both from the National Tourist Offices and in guidebooks. For information on pousadas, write to ENATUR, Avda. Santa Joana Princesa 10A, Lisbon (tel. 889078). An American company publishes a guide to pousadas and paradores: Ballard's Travel Guides, P.O. Box 647, Gig Harbor, WA 98335. If you wish to book a room in advance, you can do it through a New York booking service called Marketing Ahead (tel. 212/686-9213).

Transportation
Public transportation on the Iberian peninsula is generally slower, less frequent, and less efficient than in northern Europe. The one saving grace is that it's cheaper.

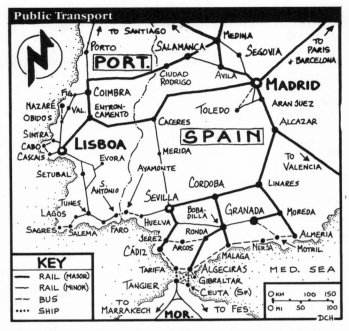

Train fares are figured by the kilometer. Second-class trains cost about $.05 a mile, while first-class ones cost about $.07 a mile. Faster trains (Talgo, Inter-City, Ter and Expreso) add on a *suplemento*. Most overnight trains have couchettes (sleeping berths, called *coche-litera*) that cost about $10. A *coche-cama*, or private berth, in a classy double compartment costs about $15. Buy these when you buy your ticket.

The Spanish rail system issues a 15-day "RENFE Tarjeta Turística" train pass, which costs about US$210 for first class and US$150 for second class. This can be a great value, and I'd pay the extra for the less crowded, more comfortable first class.

A three-week Eurailpass costs $398 (first class) and would only pay for itself on this tour if you're traveling to Spain from the north. It is a real convenience, however, not to have to buy tickets as you go. This tour, though, uses lots of buses, and Eurail is worthless on them. Also, even Eurail travelers must make reservations for longer rides. It's best to reserve your departing train on arrival in a town at the station or at a RENFE office in the town center. Keep your reservation slips until you leave the station at your destination.

The Spanish train company, RENFE, categorizes its trains as very slow (*Correo*) mail trains, pretty slow (*Tranvias* and *Semidirectos*), fast (*Expreso* and *Rapido*), and super luxury (*Ter, Electro*, and *Talgo*). These get more expensive as they pick up speed, but all are much cheaper than their northern European counterparts.

Portugal doesn't have the same categories as Spain—mostly just slow milk-run trains and an occasional Expreso. Portuguese buses are often a better transportation bet.

Since trains in Spain are often late, telephone the stations to confirm departure times. Remember, you may arrive an hour after a train has left—according to the schedule—and still catch it. Use these train station information numbers:

Barcelona 322-4142
Granada 233408
Madrid 552-0518, 276-3044, or 733-3000
Málaga 213122
Salamanca 225742
Sevilla 228817
Toledo 221272

For the complete schedule and explanation of the Spanish train system, pick up the "Grandes Relaciones Guía RENFE," available for a dollar at any train station. The "Trenes Entre Ciudades" is shorter, free, and easier to find. When reading schedules, remember: in Spain *Salidas* means departures, *Llegadas* is arrivals; in Portugal *Partidas* and *Chegadas* are departures and arrivals.

Buses will take you where the trains don't—your best bet for small towns. They vary a lot in speed and are at least as cheap as the trains ($1.00/20 miles). Remember, the price of public transportation on Sundays and holidays is greatly reduced.

In Portugal, *Paragem* = bus stop. In the countryside, stop buses by waving.

Taxis are very cheap everywhere. Use them, but insist on the meter.

Driving in Iberia is great, although major roads can be clogged by endless caravans of slow-moving trucks. Car rental is as cheap as anywhere in Europe—$150/week with unlimited mileage through your U.S.A. travel agent or on the spot over there. All you need is your American driver's license. Remember, drive very defensively. If you have an accident, you'll be blamed and are in for a monumental headache. Seatbelts are required by law. Gas and diesel prices are controlled and the same everywhere. In Iberia, *gasolina* is either *normal* or *super*. Diesel is *gasoleo*. Gas will cost you around $3 per gallon. Diesel is cheaper than gas. Expect to be stopped by the police for a routine check. (Be sure your car insurance form is up to date.) Portugal requires an International Driver's License, available quick and cheap at your hometown AAA office.

Choose a parking place carefully and never leave valuables in the car. You'll hear parking attendants constantly warning people, *"Nada en el coche"* —nothing in the car.

Privacy is a rare commodity for the Romeos and Juliets of Spain and Portugal. With so many very crowded apartments, young Iberian lovers can only "borrow the car." Outside of any big city you'll find viewpoints and other romantic parking places clogged with steamy-windowed Spanish-made Fiats nearly every night. Not a good place for sightseeing.

Recommended Guidebooks

This small book is your itinerary planner. To thoroughly enjoy and appreciate these three busy weeks, you may want supplemental information found in a directory-type guidebook. Sure, it hurts to spend $30 or $40 on extra guidebooks, but when you consider the improvements they will make in your $2,000 vacation—not to mention the money they'll save you— not buying them would be perfectly "penny-wise and pound-foolish." Here is my recommended guidebook strategy:

General low-budget, directory-type guidebooks—The best I've found are *Let's Go: Spain, Portugal and Morocco* and the *Rough Guides* to Spain and Portugal. *Let's Go*, updated each year by Harvard students, is a spinoff of the great *Let's Go: Europe* guidebook. Its approach is rather hip, youthful, and train-oriented. If you've got $30 a day for room and board, you may be a little rich for some of its recommendations, but, especially if you're going to Morocco, it's the best information source around. ($11.95, 610 pp., new editions come out each February, ISBN 0-312022-39-5.) Mark Ellingham has written very practical *Rough Guides* to both Spain and Portugal. These are written for the British market (prices are in pounds) and though hard to find in the United States, are well worth chasing down. Ellingham has an excellent command of both cultures and provides a wealth of good information. (*Spain*, ISBN 0-710203-44-6, *Portugal*, ISBN 0-710209-67-3, each $11.95.) The *Rough Guides* are not as fresh as *Let's Go*, which is updated annually.

Older travelers like the style of Arthur Frommer's *Spain and Portugal on $30 a Day*. Fodor's guides ignore alternatives that enable travelers to save money by dirtying their fingers in the local culture and are not very practical for my style of travel.

Cultural and sightseeing guides—*Michelin's Green Guides* for Spain and Portugal are great for information on the sights and culture, though they contain nothing on room and board. They are written with the driver in mind (on Michelin tires, of course). Of all the books I mention, only the Michelin guides are available in Europe; in fact, they're even cheaper in Spain than in the United States. Michener's *Iberia* is great pretrip reading for background in the area's culture. The *American Express Guide* to Spain (by Bailey Livesey, ISBN 0-130251-31-3, $9.95) is also good. The encyclopedic *Blue Guides* to Spain and Portugal are dry and scholastic but just right for some people.

Maps—Michelin makes the best. They're available and inexpensive throughout Iberia.

Rick Steves's books—Finally, I've written this book assuming you have or will read the latest edition of my book on the skills of budget travel, *Europe Through the Back Door*. To keep this "22 Days" book pocket-sized, I've resisted the temptation to repeat the most applicable and important information already included in *Europe Through the Back Door*; there is virtually no overlap.

Europe Through the Back Door gives you the basic skills, the foundation that makes this demanding 22-day plan possible. There are chapters on minimizing jet lag, packing light, driving or train travel, finding budget beds without reservations, changing money, theft and the tourist, hurdling the language barrier, health, travel photography, long-distance telephoning in Europe, travelers' toilet trauma, ugly-Americanism, laundry, and itinerary strategies and techniques that are so very important.

Europe 101: History and Art for the Traveler (co-written with Gene Openshaw) gives you the story of Europe's people, history, and art, preparing you to understand the sights of Iberia—from Roman times through the Inquisition and up to the Civil War.

Mona Winks: Self-Guided Tours of Europe's Top Museums (also co-written with Gene Openshaw) has a chapter outlining the best three-hour visit to Madrid's overwhelming Prado Museum.

Your bookstore should have these three books. They are also available directly from John Muir Publications, P.O. Box 613, Santa Fe, NM 87504, (505) 982-4078.

Apart from books, a traveler's best friends are the tourist offices you'll find throughout Spain and Portugal. Use them—for things like maps, accommodations, where to find a pharmacy, driving instructions, and recommendations for nightlife.

BACK DOOR TRAVEL PHILOSOPHY

AS TAUGHT IN *EUROPE THROUGH THE BACK DOOR*

Travel is intensified living—maximum thrills per minute and one of the last great sources of legal adventure. In many ways, the less you spend the more you get.

Experiencing the real thing requires candid informality—going "Through the Back Door."

Affording travel is a matter of priorities. Many people who "can't afford a trip" could sell their car and travel for two years.

You can travel anywhere in the world for $30 a day plus transportation costs. Money has little to do with enjoying your trip. In fact, in many ways, the less you spend the more you get—spending more money only builds a thicker wall between you and what you came to see.

A tight budget forces you to travel "close to the ground," meeting and communicating with the people, not relying on service with a purchased smile. Never sacrifice sleep, nutrition, safety, or cleanliness in the name of budget. Simply enjoy the local-style alternatives to expensive hotels and restaurants.

Extroverts have more fun. If your trip is low on magic moments, kick yourself and start making things happen. Dignity and good travel don't mix. Leave your beeper at home. Let your hair down.

If you don't enjoy a place, it's often because you don't know enough about it. Seek out the truth. Recognize tourist traps.

A culture is legitimized by its existence. Give a people the benefit of your open mind. Think of things as different but not better or worse.

Of course, travel, like the world, is a series of hills and valleys. Be fanatically positive and militantly optimistic.

Travel is addicting. It can make you a happier American, as well as a citizen of the world. Our Earth is home to five billion equally important people. That's wonderfully humbling.

Globe-trotting destroys ethnocentricity and encourages the understanding and appreciation of various cultures. Travel changes people. Many travelers toss aside their "hometown blinders," assimilating the best points of different cultures into their own character.

The world is a cultural garden. We're working on the ultimate salad. Won't you join us?

DAYS 1, 2 and 3   Arrive in Madrid, shift into Spanish gear (late meals, siestas), habla un poco español, and see the major sights of Spain's major city. With a world-class royal palace, the Prado Museum and flea market, and enough street-singing, barhopping, people-watching vitality to give any visitor a boost of youth, Madrid is the place to start your three-week Iberian adventure.

DAY 4   Spain's history is lavish, brutal, and complicated. Tour the imposing El Escorial palace, sternly elegant and steeped in history. Then pay tribute to the countless victims of Spain's Civil War at the awesome Valley of the Fallen before setting up in Segovia to enjoy its Roman aqueduct, its cathedral and a succulent roast pig.

DAY 5   Next it's on into Portugal, stopping for a few interesting breaks. Grab a quick look at the graceful architecture and magnificent Plaza Mayor of Salamanca, explore the medieval turrets and crannies of little Ciudad Rodrigo and finish the day in Portugal's prestigious university town of Coimbra.

DAY 6   After a few hours in Portugal's "Oxford," drop by the patriotic pride and architectural joy of Portugal, the Batalha Church. If the spirit moves you, the pilgrimage site at Fatima is just down the road. Find a hotel at nearby Nazaré, an Atlantic Coast fishing town that reeks with tradition while comfortably accommodating its visitors. Fill yourself with shrimp.

DAY 7   After all the traveling you've done, it's high time for an easy day and some fun in the Portuguese sun. Your beach town, surrounded by cork groves, eucalyptus trees, ladies who wear seven petticoats, and men who stow their cigarettes and fish hooks in their stocking hats, offers the perfect mix of sun, sand, and seafood, with enough salty fishing village atmosphere to make you pucker.

DAYS 8 and 9   After a stop at the almost edibly cute walled town of Obidos, plunge into Portugal's capital and largest city, Lisbon. The closest thing to an urban jungle on this trip, Lisbon is a yellowed scrapbook of trolleys, sailors' quarters, mournful folk music, and Old World elegance caked in twentieth-century squalor. There's plenty to see, do, eat, and drink.

Tour Route

DAY 10   Take a side trip from Lisbon directly into Portugal's seafaring glory days. After a morning of royal coaches, elegant cloisters, and maritime memories in the suburb of Belem, you'll head for the hills to climb through the Versailles of Portugal, the Pena Palace. Then, after a romp along the ruined ramparts of a deserted Moorish castle on a neighboring hilltop and a short walk out to Portugal's wind-lashed westernmost point, you'll finish the day dining, gambling, or strolling along the beachfront promenade of the well-worn resort towns of Cascais or Estoril.

DAYS 11 and 12   After big-city Lisbon, you'll enjoy a day and a half in a sleepy fishing village on the south coast and a chance to linger longer on Portugal's best beach. Your Algarve hideaway is sunny Salema. It's just you, a handful of fishermen, your wrinkled landlady, and a few other globe-trotting experts in lethargy. Nearby sightseeing possibilities include Cape Sagres, Europe's "Land's End" and home of Henry the Navigator's famous navigation school, and the jet-setty resort of Portimão. Or you could just work on a tan and see how slow you can get your pulse in sleepy Salema.

DAYS 13 and 14   Roll up your beach towel, it's time to meander across the Algarve, catch the tiny ferry into Spain, and experience Sevilla. The city of Carmen, flamenco, Don Giovanni, and the 1992 World's Fair has its share of impressive sights, but its real magic is in its ambience: its quietly tangled Jewish Quarter, riveting flamenco shows, thriving bars, and teeming paseo. Spend your evening in the streets, rafting through a choppy river of Spanish humanity.

DAYS 15 and 16   Leave Sevilla early to wind through the golden hills of the "Ruta de Pueblos Blancos" in search of Andalusia's most exotic whitewashed villages. After a night in the region's romantic capital, Arcos de la Frontera, and a leisurely morning exploring Arcos, dipping into other friendly and forgotten hill towns, or savoring a sherry tour in Jerez, it's on to the least-touristy piece of Spain's generally over-touristy south coast: the whitewashed, almost Arabic-flavored port of Tarifa.

DAY 17   Ooo Morocco! For something entirely different, take the hydrofoil day trip from Tarifa to Tangiers. Admittedly, Tangiers is the Tijuana of Morocco, but the excellent one-day tour from Tarifa will fill your day with a whirlpool of carpets, tea, belly dancers, fake silver dollars, donkey dust, and camel snorts. This kind of cultural voyeurism is almost like visiting the devil, but it's nonstop action and as memorable as an audit.

DAY 18   After your day in Africa, a day in England may sound jolly good. And that's just where you're going today—to the land of tea and scones, fish and chips, pubs and bobbies—Gibraltar. Following this splash of uncharacteristically sunny England, enter the bikini-strangled land of basted bodies on the beach, the Costa del Sol. Bed down in this congested region's closest thing to pleasant, the happy town of Nerja, for a first-hand look at Europe's beachy playground.

DAYS 19 and 20   After a beach-easy morning on the Costa del Sol and a crawl through the stalagmighty Nerja caves, say "adiós" to the Mediterranean and head into the rugged Sierra Nevada mountains to the historic city of Granada. Famous as the last stronghold of the Moorish kingdom, Granada has the incomparable Alhambra palace and an exotically tangled Arab quarter. After a day and a half here, you'll know why they say, "There's nothing crueler than being blind in Granada."

DAYS 21 and 22   After the 250-mile trip north among the windmills and castles of La Mancha and dusty memories of Don

Quixote, you'll enter the historic, artistic, and spiritual capital of Spain, Toledo. Incredibly well preserved and full of cultural wonder, the entire city has been declared a national historical monument. Toledo teems with tourists, souvenirs, and great art by day, delicious roast suckling pig, echoes of El Greco, and medieval magic by night. It's a great finale for your 22 days in Spain and Portugal. You're just an hour south of your trip's starting point—Madrid. *Adiós!*

ARRIVE IN MADRID

You lose a day flying to Europe: if you leave on a Tuesday, you'll land on Wednesday. Today will be spent getting acquainted with Madrid and finding a room for your three-night stay.

On this first day in Madrid, you'll be set up by evening, enjoying a relaxing dinner and resting up for sightseeing the next day. If you just landed, jet lag will lower its sleepy boom on you too early. An evening walk is a cool, enjoyable, breathe-deep way to stay awake until a reasonable bedtime for your first night in Europe.

Suggested Schedule

> Depart U.S.A.
> Arrive at Madrid airport or train station.
> Bus, subway, or taxi to the very central Puerta del Sol.
> Find your hotel, orient in old town. Have a late dinner—tapas.

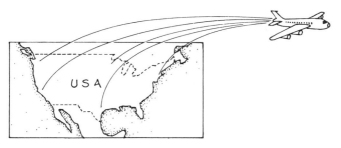

Depart U.S.A.
Call before going to the airport to confirm departure time as scheduled. Bring something—a book, a journal, some handwork, an infant—to keep yourself occupied in the event of delays. Remember, no matter how long it takes, flying to Europe is a very easy way to get there. If you arrived in one piece on the day you hoped to, the trip is a smashing success.

To minimize jet lag:
■ Leave well rested. Pretend you are leaving a day earlier than you really are. Plan accordingly and enjoy a peaceful last day.

■ During the flight, minimize stress by eating lightly, avoiding alcohol, caffeine, and sugar. Say, "Two orange juices, no ice, please," every chance you get. Take walks.

■ After boarding the plane, set your watch ahead to European time: start adjusting mentally before you land.

■ Sleep through the in-flight movie—or at least close your eyes and fake it.

■ On the day you arrive, keep yourself awake until a reasonable local bedtime. A long evening city walk is helpful.

■ You'll probably wake up very early the next morning—but ready to roll.

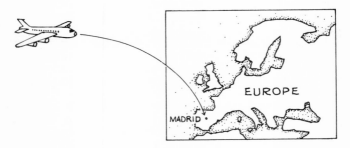

Arrival

Madrid's Barajas Airport is ten miles east of downtown. Like most European airports, it has a bank that keeps long hours and offers fair exchange rates. There are also a tourist desk (English speaking, helpful, with free Madrid map and room information), on-the-spot car rental agencies and easy public transportation into town. Airport taxis are notoriously expensive. Take the yellow bus into Madrid. It leaves about four times an hour for Plaza Colón ($2, 20-minute ride).

If you're arriving by train from France or Barcelona, you'll land at the modern Chamartin Station. While you're at the station, make a reservation for your departure. (Long train rides in Spain require reservations, even with a Eurailpass.) Then catch the metro (requiring one change of lines) to metro stop "Sol." Taxis are reasonable from the station.

Car rental: if at all possible, don't drive in Madrid. Rent your car when you're ready to leave. Ideally, you should make car rental arrangements through your travel agent before you leave. In Madrid, try Europacar (García de Paredes 12), Hertz (Gran Vía 80) or Avis (Gran Vía 60, tel. 457-9706).

Orientation

Madrid is the hub of Spain. This modern capital, with a population of four million, is young by European standards. Only 400
years ago, King Philip II decided to move the capital of his
empire from Toledo to Madrid. One hundred years ago, Madrid
had only 300,000 people, so while nine-tenths of the city is
modern sprawl, the historic center can be covered easily
on foot.

Today's Madrid is upbeat and vibrant, enjoying a kind of
renaissance. You'll feel it. It's a proud city that now looks to an
exciting future as well as its rich past. As a visitor, your time will
be divided between the city's artistic and historic treasures and
its busy barhopping, car-honking, skyscraping contemporary
scene.

The Puerta del Sol is dead center. In fact, this is even considered the center of Spain: notice the kilometer zero marker, from
which all of Spain is surveyed, at the police station. An east-
west axis from the Royal Palace to the Prado Museum and Retiro
Park cuts the historic center in half.

North of the Puerta del Sol, the Gran Vía runs east and west.
Between the Gran Vía and the Puerta del Sol are pedestrian
shopping streets. The Gran Vía, bubbling with business, expensive shops, and cinemas, leads down to the impressively modern Plaza de España. North of the Gran Vía is the fascinating
Malasana quarter with its colorful small houses, shoemaker's
shops, sleazy-looking hombres, milk vendors, bars, and cheap
hotels.

To the southwest of the Puerta del Sol is an older district
(sixteenth-century) with the slow-down-and-smell-the-
cobbles Plaza Mayor and plenty of relics from preindustrial
Spain. In the Lavapies quarter (southeast of Plaza Mayor) notice
the names of the streets: Calles de Cuchilleros (knifesmiths),
Laterones (brass-casters), Bordaderos (embroiderers), Tinteros
(dyers), Curtideros (tanners).

East of the Puerta del Sol is Madrid's huge museum (Prado),
huge park (Retiro), and tiny river (Manzanares). Just north of the
park is the elegant Salamanca quarter.

Accommodations

Madrid has plenty of centrally located budget hotels and pensions. Cabs are cheap. On arrival downtown, I'd take one to the
Puerta del Sol and wander generally south and east. Doorbells
line each building entrance. Push one that says "*Pension*."
You'll have no trouble finding a decent double for $15 to $30.
(Remember this book's hotel double room price categories:
cheap—under $17; inexpensive—$17-$30; moderate—$30-$50;

expensive—over $50.) It's most crowded in July and August.

Choose small streets. The rooms get cheaper—and seedier—
as you approach the Atocha Station. Below are hotels clustered
in three particularly good areas.

Gran Vía: The pulse of today's Madrid is best felt along the
Gran Vía. This big, busy main drag in the heart of the city is
noisier and more expensive than other areas. Ask for a quiet
room in the back of the hotel. **Hostal Residencia Miami** is
clean, quiet, cheery, with lovely rooms, mirrors, and plastic
flower decor throughout. It's like staying at your eccentric
aunt's in Miami Beach. The bubbly landlady, Mrs. Sanz, and her
husband are very friendly but speak very little English (inexpensive, Gran Vía 44, eighth floor [elevator], 28013 Madrid, tel.
521-1464). In the same building, with higher prices, less charm,
more English and no pink flamingos, you'll find **Hostal
Residencia Continental** (inexpensive, tel. 521-4640), and
Hostal Residencia Valencia (inexpensive, tel. 522-1115). My
choice for a Gran Vía splurge is **Hostal Salas** with a nice lounge
and a good location (moderate, English spoken, Gran Vía 38,
fifth floor, tel. 231-9600).

Prado: Just across from the Prado Museum, you'll find two
very good places. **Hotel Sud-Americana** (inexpensive, Paseo

del Prado 12, sixth floor, tel. 429-2564) and **Hostal Residencia Coruna** (inexpensive, Paseo del Prado 12, third floor, tel. 429-2543) are clean and friendly, though they come with some traffic noise. The staff speaks a little English.

Piazza Santa Ana: Piazza Santa Ana has plenty of small, pleasant, and cheap places. It's my favorite Madrid locale for its almost Parisian ambience, colorful bars, and very central location—just off Puerta del Sol, three minutes to the right of the "Tío Pepe" sign on Espoz y Mina. **Hostal Filo** is squeaky clean with a nervous but helpful management, no English, but a tremendous value (inexpensive, Plaza de Santa Ana 15, second floor, tel. 522-4056). **Hostal Iruna** is smaller than Filo but has big, bright, and clean rooms. Carmina, the fun landlady, speaks un poco English (get her talking—she loves to shock you with her dirty English vocabulary) but loves the United States and normally has "American-speakers" around (cheap, Plaza de Santa Ana 15, third floor, tel. 521-0241).

Decent places right on the Puerta del Sol are **Pension Marimart** (14, moderate, tel. 222-9815) and **Pension Sol** (9, moderate).

Madrid has two good youth hostels. **Santa Cruz de Marcenado** (Calle Santa Cruz de Marcenado 28, tel. 247-4532), near metro stop "Arguelles," is clean and well run, in a student neighborhood, cheap, but has a 12:30 curfew. There's also youth hostel **Richard Schirrman** (Casa de Campo, tel. 463-5699) near metro stop "El Lago." Since hotels and *hostales* (Spanish-style hotels, not to be confused with youth hostels) are so inexpensive in Madrid, I'd skip the youth hostels.

Food
Madrid loves to eat well. In Spain, only Barcelona rivals Madrid for taste bud thrills. You have two basic dining choices: an atmospheric sit-down meal in a well-chosen restaurant, or a potentially more atmospheric mobile meal doing the popular "tapa tango"—a local tradition of going from one bar to the next munching, drinking, and socializing. Tapas are small appetizers, salads, and deep-fried foods served in most bars. Dining is not cheap. Tapas are—and Madrid is Spain's tapa capital.

Some good sit-down splurge restaurants are: **Zalacaín**, Alvaraz de Baena 4, closed Sundays and all of August, quite expensive, with garden and terrace; **El Amparo**, Callejón de Puigcerda 8, closed Sundays and August; and **Jockey**, Amador de los Ríos 6, also closed Sundays and August. Also good are: **Casa Lucio**, Cava Baja 35 in old town; **El Schotis**, Cava Baja 7, closed Sundays and August; **Restaurante La Villa de Luarca**, Concepción Arenal 6, just off Gran Vía; and **Lhardy**, near Puerta del

Sol at Carrera de San Jeronimo 8, for great tapas downstairs and classy nineteenth-century atmosphere upstairs. Restaurants don't get crowded until after 22:00.

Most Americans are drawn to Hemingway's favorite, **Sobrinos del Botín** (Cuchilleros 17 in old town). It's frighteningly touristy. Good vegetarian food is served at **La Galette** (Conda de Aranda 11, near the archaeology museum). Your hotel receptionist is a reliable source for more information.

A good tapas district is the area just north of Glorieta de Bilbao. Just off Piazza Santa Ana, Calle de Manuel Fernandez y Gonzalez has great bars. For tapa bars, try this route: from Puerta del Sol, head east along Carrera de San Jeronimo, then branch off onto Calles de la Cruz, Echegaray, del Pozo, and Nuñez del Arce.

At Carrera San Jeronimo 6, the atmospheric **Museo del Jamón** ("'museum of ham'"—note the tasty decor, with smoked ham and sausage lining the ceiling) is a fun, cheap stand-up bar with good bocadillos and raciones. An atmospheric place to assemble a cheap picnic is the Mercado de San Miguel near the Puerta del Sol corner of the Plaza Mayor.

The **Restaurant Bar El Fijón de Benavente**, at Plaza del Angel 1 (toward Plaza Mayor from Plaza Santa Ana), has friendly service, great paella, and lots of sangría.

Each night the Malasana quarter around the Plaza Dos de Mayo erupts with street life. Madrid's new bohemian, intellectual, liberal scene has flowered only since the death of Franco. Artists, actors, former exiles, and Madrid's youth gather here. **Pepe Botella** is a fun restaurant, and tapa bars abound in this district. Try the old **Café Gijón** (Paseo de Recoletos 21), **Comercial** (Glorieta de Bilbao 10, north of Manuela Malasana), or **Bocaccio**. Single women should probably avoid this rowdy neighborhood.

The top ice cream shops are at Calles Goya 68, Barcalo 1, Tirso de Molina 9, Magallanes 13, and Lopez de Hoyos 106.

Helpful Hints

Madrid's subway—cheap (50 ptas) and simple—is understandably the pride of the Spanish public transportation system. Madrid's broad streets can be hot and exhausting. A subway trip of even a stop or two can save time and energy. Once you're underground, helpful signs show the number of the line and the direction it's headed (e.g., "1-Portazgo"). Directions are indicated by end-of-the-line stops. Subways run from 6:00 to 1:30. Pick up a free map ("Plano del Metro") at any station. The Atocha and Chamartin train stations are easily connected by subway.

City buses are not so cheap or easy but still good. Get details and schedules at the booth on Puerta del Sol.

Plan ahead. If you're returning to Madrid at the end of your trip, make a reservation at the hotel of your choice. If you pay in advance, you can arrive as late as you like. You can also leave anything you won't need in the hotel's storage closet free (mark your name and return date on it clearly). You may also want to reserve rooms now for Segovia and Toledo, which can be crowded in July and August. Do what you can in Madrid to smooth out your travel plans.

Madrid's main tourist information office is at Plaza Mayor 3 (Monday through Friday 10:00-13:30, 16:00-19:00, Saturday 10:00-13:30, tel. 266-5477), with other offices on Plaza España, in train stations, and at the airport. Pick up a free city map and list of accommodations, confirm your sightseeing plans and hours, and leaf through their handy English-language monthly newsletter *En Madrid*. Another good periodical entertainment guide, *Guía del Ocio*, is available at any kiosk.

The Madrid tourist office can give you information (especially maps) on other Spanish cities you'll be visiting. Pick up what you can; many small town offices keep erratic hours, and it's very helpful to have this information as you approach a new town.

The U.S. Embassy is at Serrano 75 (tel. 091/276-3600 or, for emergencies, 091/276-3229).

SIGHTSEE IN MADRID

For two days you'll dive headlong into the historic grandeur and intimate charms of Spain's capital. The lavish Royal Palace, which rivals Versailles, comes with a fine tour. Madrid's huge Retiro Park invites you for a shady siesta and a hopscotch through a mosaic of lovers, families, skateboarders, pet walkers, and old-time bench-sitters.

You'll need plenty of time for Madrid's teeming flea market, cheering bullfight arena, elegant shops, and very people-friendly pedestrian zones. The canvas highlights of the great Prado Museum, such as Picasso's stirring *Guernica*, are a must.

Suggested Schedule	
Day 2	
9:30	Be at the Royal Palace when it opens. Tour palace, armory, pharmacy, library.
13:00	Lunch and siesta.
16:00	Browse, stroll, shop the Gran Vía and Plaza Mayor areas.
Note:	Try to be in Madrid on a Sunday for Europe's best flea market, El Rastro, in the morning and a bullfight in the evening.
Day 3	
9:00	Options, trip planning or possible El Escorial side trip.
11:00	People-watch and picnic in Retiro Park.
13:00	*Guernica*.
14:00	Tour Europe's greatest collection of paintings, the Prado.

Sightseeing Highlights
▲▲▲ **Prado Museum**—The Prado is my favorite art museum. With over 3,000 paintings, including rooms of masterpieces by Velázquez, Goya, El Greco, and Bosch, it's overwhelming. Take a tour or buy a guidebook. Focus on the Flemish and Northern art (Bosch, Dürer, Rubens); the Italian collection (Fra Angelico, Raphael, Botticelli, Titian); and the Spanish art (El Greco, Velázquez, Goya).

Follow Goya through his cheery (*The Parasol*), political (*The Third of May*), and dark (*Saturn Devouring His Children*) stages. In each stage, Goya asserted his independence from artis-

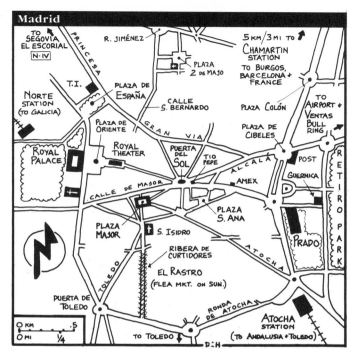

tic conventions. Even the standard court portraits of the "first" stage reflect his politically liberal viewpoint, subtly showing the vanity and stupidity of his subjects by the look in their goony eyes. His political stage, with paintings like *The Third of May*, depicting a massacre of Spaniards by Napoleon's troops, makes him one of the first artists with a social conscience. Finally, in his gloomy "dark stage," Goya probed the inner world of fears and nightmares, anticipating the twentieth-century preoccupation with dreams.

Also, don't miss Bosch's ("El Bosco" in Spanish) *Garden of Delights*. The Prado has a good cafeteria and a great print and book shop. You can visit twice in one day with the same ticket. Open 9:00-19:00, Sundays 9:00-14:00, closed Mondays. The quietest time is lunchtime—from 14:00 to 15:00.

▲▲ **Picasso's *Guernica***—Located in the Casón de Buen Retiro, three blocks east of the Prado, this famous antiwar painting deserves much study. The death of Franco ended the work's American exile and now it reigns as Spain's national piece of art—behind bulletproof glass. Your Prado ticket is good here; same hours as the Prado.

▲ **Plaza Mayor**—This vast, cobbled traffic-free chunk of seventeenth-century Spain is just a short walk from the Puerta del Sol. A stamp and coin market bustles on Sunday mornings, and any day it's a colorful place to enjoy a cup of coffee.

▲▲ **Royal Palace (Palacio Real)**—Europe's third-greatest palace (after Versailles and Vienna) is packed with tourists. An English tour of its lavish interior is included—and required. Open Monday-Saturday 9:30-12:45, 16:00-17:45, Sundays 9:30-12:45. The nearby Museo de Carruajes Reales (same hours as the palace) has an impressive collection of royal carriages.

▲▲ **El Rastro**—This is Europe's biggest flea market, a field day for people-watchers. The hours are Sundays 9:00-14:00 (smaller versions on Fridays and Saturdays). Thousands of stalls titillate over a million browsers. If you like garage sales, you'll love El Rastro. You can buy or sell nearly anything here. Start at the Plaza Mayor and head south, or take the subway to Tirso de Molina. Hang onto your wallet. Munch on a sweet pepito or a relleno (sweet pudding-filled pastry). Europe's biggest stamp market thrives simultaneously on the Plaza Mayor.

▲ **Chapel San Antonio de la Florida**—Goya's grave sits under a splendid cupola filled with Goya frescoes. (Tuesday-Friday 10:00-14:00 and 17:00-21:00, Saturdays and Sundays 10:00-14:00.)

▲▲ **Retiro Park**—Siesta in this 350-acre green and breezy escape from the city. Rent a rowboat, have a picnic. These are peaceful gardens with great people-watching. The Botanical Garden (Jardín Botánico) nearby is a pleasant extension of the Retiro Park to the southwest.

▲▲ **Bullfight**—Madrid's Plaza de Toros (metro: "Ventas") hosts Spain's top bullfights most Sundays from Easter through October. Top fights sell out in advance, but you can generally get a ticket at the door. Fights usually start at 19:00 and are a rare example of Spanish punctuality. There are no bad seats: paying more gets you in the shade and/or closer to the gore. (Filas 8, 9, and 10 tend to be closest to the action.) Madrid and Sevilla will probably be your only chances to catch a bullfight in Spain on this tour. The bullfighting museum (Museo Taurino), open daily 10:30-13:00 and 15:30-19:00, is next to the bullring.

▲ **Plaza de España**—Modern Madrid centers around this plaza with its huge stone monument to Cervantes (with statues of Don Quixote and Sancho Panza), plenty of busy student-filled cafés, and the Edificio España skyscraper, which offers a great city view from its 25th-floor café.

Entertainment
The people of Madrid ("'Madrileños'") siesta because so much goes on in the evening. The nightly paseo is Madrid on parade.

Young and old, people are outside cruising without cars, seeing and being seen. Gran Vía and the Paseo del Prado are particularly active scenes.

You'll find live music around Plaza Dos de Mayo and jazz at **Whisky Jazz** (Diego de León 7), **Manuela** (San Vicente Ferrer 29), and **Ragtime** (Ruiz 20). Flamenco is difficult to pin down since the "in" places change very fast. Try **Arco de Cuchilleros** (Cuchilleros 7, metro: "Sol"), **Las Brujas** (Norte 15, metro: "San Bernardo," tel. 222-5325, 21:30-3:00), **Café de Chinitas** (Torija 7), **Corral de la Morerá** (Morería 7), or, better yet, ask your hotel receptionist.

For a colorful amusement park scene, try **Parque de Atracciones**, (open daily 11:00-16:00, Saturdays and Sundays 11:00-13:00, metro: "Batan"), with its Venetian canals, dancing, eating, and people watching. Visit Spain's best zoo (open 10:00-21:00). Both are in the vast Casa del Campo Park just west of the Royal Palace.

Itinerary Option
Tomorrow's plan is very tight, especially for those without a car. You may want to tour El Escorial today, taking advantage of the excellent public transportation connections from downtown Madrid (20 trains make the 30-mile trip daily), and make tomorrow very simple by skipping the Valley of the Fallen and going directly to Segovia.

EL ESCORIAL, VALLEY OF THE FALLEN, AND SEGOVIA

Pick up your rental car or catch the train. Head for the country-side to tour the brutal, but lavish, Escorial palace and the awesome underground memorial church dedicated to the victims from both sides of Spain's bloody Civil War. Set up in Segovia with time to enjoy its old center, cathedral, and castle. By dinnertime you'll be hungry enough to eat an entire roast suckling pig. Busy day. Tasty finale.

Suggested Schedule

9:00	Pick up rental car and drive northwest.
10:00	Tour El Escorial.
13:00	Lunch or picnic at Valley of the Fallen.
14:00	Tour Memorial to Victims of the Civil War.
15:00	Drive to Segovia.
16:00	Arrive in Segovia, check into hotel.
17:00	Tour Alcazar and cathedral, stroll down to aqueduct.
20:00	Roast suckling lamb or pig for dinner.

Transportation: Madrid to Segovia (50 miles)

By car, today is easy. Take a taxi to your car rental office. (Telephone the day before to confirm your reservation, and ask how early you can pick the car up.) Try to get an early start, pick up the car by 8:30, get directions to A6, and get to El Escorial by 9:30 to beat the crowds. You'll see the huge cross marking the Valley of the Fallen. From there, you climb past flocks of sheep, over a 5,000-foot-high mountain pass (Puerto de Navacerrada), and through La Granja to Segovia.

Today is already jam-packed, and Segovia is much more important than La Granja, but if you're into gardens, you might want to squeeze in a quick La Granja stop. In Segovia, park as close to the Plaza Mayor as possible.

By train, today is more difficult. Madrid offers many connections to El Escorial (20 trains daily from Atocha or Chamartin, with connecting buses from El Escorial train station to the palace) and Segovia (12 trains daily, 2-hour trip from either of Madrid's train stations). But connecting El Escorial, the Valley of the Fallen, and Segovia is more difficult. Unless you hitchhike or the tourist office in Madrid has a solution, Eurailers may want to do El Escorial as a side trip (possibly on Day 2 or 3) and train directly to Segovia from Madrid. From the Segovia train station, catch bus #3 downtown to Plaza Mayor and the tourist office.

Sightseeing Highlights near Madrid

▲▲▲ **El Escorial**—A symbol of power rather than elegance, this sixteenth-century palace 30 miles northwest of Madrid gives us a better feel for the Counter-Reformation and the Inquisition than any other building. Its construction dominated the Spanish economy for 20 years. For that reason, Madrid has almost nothing else to show from this most powerful period of Spanish history. This giant, gloomy building (gray-black stone, 2,500 windows, 200 yards long and 150 yards wide) looks more like a prison than a palace. Four hundred years ago, Philip II ruled his bulky empire and directed the Inquisition from here. It's full of history, art, and Inquisition ghosts.

The place is confusing, and private guides are good but expensive. See the church (put 100 pesetas in the light box for a spectacular illumination), mausoleum (stacked with 26 royal tombs), and monastery with the royal palace and the austere private apartments of Spain's intriguing King Phillip II. You'll see magnificent tapestries from Goya paintings now in the Prado, a great library with a thousand-year-old book of gospels printed with 17 pounds of gold-leaf letters, each cut out and pasted on with egg white glue. The "new museums" (Nuevos Museos) have some impressive paintings, including works by El Greco, Bosch, and Titian. Certain parts of El Escorial require a tour. Insist on an English one. Open 10:00-13:30 and 15:30-18:30, closed Mondays.

▲▲ **Valley of the Fallen (El Valle de los Caídos)**—Nine miles toward Segovia from El Escorial towers a 150-yard-tall granite cross marking an immense and powerful underground monument to the countless victims of Spain's twentieth-century nightmare—its Civil War (1936-1939). A solemn silence fills the memorial room, larger than Saint Peter's Basilica, as Spaniards visit the grave of General Franco. Open daily 10:00-18:00.

▲ **La Granja Palace**—This "Little Versailles," six miles south of Segovia, is much smaller and happier than El Escorial. The palace and gardens were built by the homesick French king, Phillip V, grandson of Louis XIV. It's smaller, more manageable, and much less crowded than its inspiration and is a must for tapestry lovers. Open Monday-Friday 10:00-13:30, 15:00-17:00. Fountain displays (which send local crowds into a frenzy) erupt at 17:30 on Thursdays, Saturdays, Sundays, and holidays. Entry to the palace includes a required 45-minute guided tour (English rare).

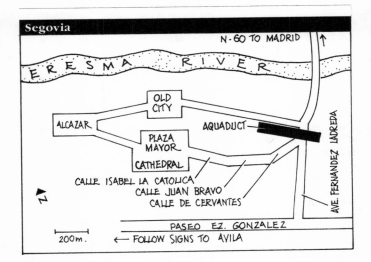

Segovia

Segovia

Segovia (elevation 3,000 ft., population 55,000), just 50 miles from Madrid, boasts a great Roman aqueduct, a cathedral, and a castle. It's your best look at Castilla, well worth the better part of a day. The tourist information office at Plaza Mayor 10 is open 9:00-14:00, sometimes 16:00-18:00, closed Sundays (tel. 911/430328).

Segovia is a medieval "ship" ready for your inspection. Start at the stern—the aqueduct—and stroll up Calle de Cervantes to the prickly Gothic masts of the cathedral. Explore the tangle of narrow streets around the Plaza Mayor, then descend to the Alcazar at the bow. To get a quick view of the city's layout, walk south from the aqueduct along Avenida de Fernandez Ladrera and climb the foothills where the city's poor live in shanties with condominium views. The most impressive view of Segovia is one mile north of town on the road to Valladolid.

Segovia's Sightseeing Highlights

▲▲ **Roman Aqueduct**—Built by the Romans, who ruled Spain for over 500 years, this 2,000-year-old *acueducto Romano* is 2,500 feet long and 100 feet high, has 118 arches, yet was made without any mortar. Climb the stairs at one end to the top of the old city wall, where you'll get a good look at the channel that carried the stream of water into the city until the beginning of this century. You'll find another good view from Plaza del Azoguejo.

▲ **Cathedral**—Segovia's cathedral was Spain's last major
Gothic building. Embellished to the hilt with pinnacles and flying buttresses, this is a great example of the final overripe stage
of Gothic called "Flamboyant." The spacious and elegant, but
dark, interior provides a delightful contrast. Admission is free;
100 pesetas gets you into the small, but interesting, museum and
the cloister. Open 10:00-19:00.

▲ **Alcazar**—This Disneyesque exaggeration of the old castle,
which burned down 100 years ago, is still fun to explore and
worthwhile for the view of the cathedral and town from the
tower. (Open 10:00-19:00, 150 pesetas.) The Throne Room (Sala
del Solio), where Isabel was crowned and Columbus came to
get his fantasy financed, is a must. Very helpful private English
tours are available on request for 100 pesetas per person.

Avila—A popular side trip from Madrid, this town has perfectly
preserved medieval walls (to climb them, enter through the
gardens of the parador) and several fine churches and monasteries. It's just beyond El Escorial; you could do them together in
one day, spending the night in Avila and carrying on to Segovia
(four buses daily) or Salamanca (four trains daily). The tourist
office (open 9:30-13:30 and 16:00-19:00) is opposite the cathedral on the main plaza. Pick up a box of the famous local sweets
called *yemas*.

Accommodations

Look near the Plaza Mayor or the aqueduct. **Hotel Acueducto**
(inexpensive, Avenida Padre Claret 10) is a modern-style refuge
in this busy area near the aqueduct. The Plaza Mayor is quieter
and more central. **Hostal Victoria** (inexpensive, Plaza Mayor 5,
tel. 435711, right on the main square) offers surprisingly quiet,
basic rooms. The **Hostal Juan Bravo** (inexpensive, at Calle
Juan Bravo 12, tel. 435521) is central, clean, and bright, but
there is no English spoken. **Plaza Hostal Residencia** (inexpensive, Cronista Lecea 11, tel. 431228) is very central, just off
Plaza Mayor. It, too, is clean, friendly, and cozy. Call Jose Antonio for reservations a day in advance of arrival. **Hotel Los
Linajes** (expensive, at Dr. Valasco 9, tel. 911/431712) is very
classy, central, and rustic, with views and modern niceties, in
the old center near the Alcazar. The **Segovia Youth Hostel** (on
Paseo Conde de Sepulvedra between the train and bus stations,
tel. 420027, closed mid-August to mid-September) is a great
hostel—easygoing, comfortable, clean, friendly, and very
cheap. Segovia is crowded in July and August, so arrive early or
call ahead.

Food

Roast suckling pig (*cochinillo asado*) and lamb, Segovia's culi-
nary claims to fame, are well worth a splurge here (or in Toledo
or Salamanca). The **Mesón de Candido** (Plaza del Azoguejo 5,
near the aqueduct) is one of the top restaurants in Castile—
famous, good, and overpriced. Also very good is **Casa Amado**
at Ladieda 9. The best bars and nightlife cluster around Plaza
Mayor. Try those on Calle de Infantes Isabella, especially the
very local and busy **Mesón del Campesino** (cheap menu del
día). Cheaper and just as good are **La Oficina** (Cronista Lecea
10, just off Plaza Mayor), **Jose María** (Cronista Lecea 13), and
Tasca la Posada (Judería Vieja 5).

SALAMANCA TO COIMBRA, PORTUGAL

Today, with the help of a time change in our favor, we'll take a quick look at Spain's "City of Grace," Salamanca, then explore the medieval turrets and crannies of Ciudad Rodrigo, and cross into Portugal to set up in its prestigious university town of Coimbra.

Suggested Schedule

8:00	Depart for Salamanca.
10:00	See Salamanca center, Plaza Mayor, cathedral, university.
12:30	Lunch in Salamanca.
14:00	Continue on.
15:00	Ciudad Rodrigo. Wander old town, climb the wall.
16:00	Drive into Portugal (set watch back one hour at border).
19:00	Arrive Coimbra, find hotel and dinner.

Transportation

Segovia to Salamanca (100 miles): In the afternoon, we'll start the easy two-hour drive to Salamanca with a chance to see the famous medieval walls of Avila en route. Drive south from the aqueduct on Avenida Fernandez Ladreda and follow the Avila signs. Just after the abandoned ghost church at Villacastin, turn onto N501.

When you arrive in Salamanca, park your car south of the Puente Nuevo (new bridge) and leave it. Parking is difficult, and the town is small enough to manage on foot.

Segovia has plenty of thieves. Leave nothing of value in your car—especially in large, tourist-area car parks.

Public transportation from Segovia to Salamanca is messy, so if you're traveling without a car, consider seeing Segovia as a half-day side trip from Madrid and going directly from Madrid to Salamanca. There are 12 buses a day from Madrid (4 ½ hours). The train (3 ½ hours) leaves four times a day from Madrid's Príncipe Pío Station, via Avila (8:40, 9:25, 15:40, 19:10). The Salamanca train station is an easy bus ride or a 15-minute walk from Plaza Mayor (train information: tel. 225742).

Salamanca to Ciudad Rodrigo (60 miles): An easy, boring, but fast drive. There are six buses a day, but from Ciudad

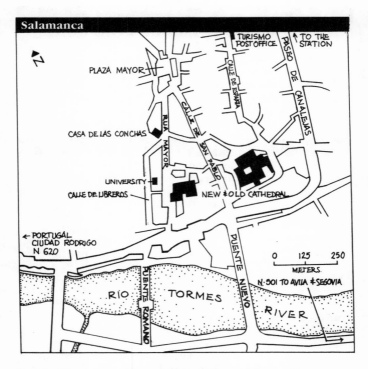

Rodrigo the connection to the border is terrible—only one a
day. Five trains a day go from Salamanca through Ciudad
Rodrigo and Guentes de Onoro to Guarda. There are good connections from Guarda to Coimbra and Lisbon.

Ciudad Rodrigo to Coimbra (150 miles): The drive is fast,
easy, uncrowded and, until Guarda, fairly dull. After Guarda, the
road winds you through the beautiful Serra da Estrela mountains. Expect no hassles at the border. Remember to set your
watch back one hour as you cross into Portugal. All in all, the
drive from Salamanca to Coimbra takes five or six hours. Park
the car and leave it (Coimbra is an "on foot" town) along the
river on Avenida Emidio Navarro. Leave absolutely *nothing*
inside.

There are five trains daily from Ciudad Rodrigo to Coimbra
(two come directly from Paris, and three require a change in
Guarda). The bus station is a mile from the center down Avenida
Fernao Magalhaes. Six or seven buses leave Rodrigo daily for
Spain or Lisbon.

Salamanca Sightseeing Highlights

▲▲▲ **Plaza Mayor**—*The* Spanish plaza, this central square, built in 1755, is really the best in Spain. It's a fine place to nurse a cup of coffee, watch the world go by, and imagine the excitement of the days when bullfights were held in this square.

▲▲ **Cathedral**—This is actually two cathedrals, both richly ornamented, side by side. The "new" cathedral was begun in 1513, with Renaissance and Baroque parts added later. The old cathedral goes way back to the twelfth century. (Open 10:00-13:45, 16:00-19:00.)

▲▲ **University**—Founded in 1230, Salamanca University is the oldest in Spain and was one of Europe's leading centers of learning for 400 years. Columbus came here for help with his nautical calculations, and today many Americans enjoy its excellent summer program. Open Monday-Saturday, 9:30-13:30, 16:00-18:00. Explore the old lecture halls where many of Spain's Golden Age heroes studied. The entrance portal is a great example of Spain's "Plateresque" style—masonry so intricate it looks like silver work.

Salamanca's Blood Red Graffiti—As you walk through the old town or by the cathedrals, you may see red writing on the walls. For centuries, students have celebrated receiving their Ph.D.'s by killing and roasting a bull, having a big feast, and writing their names and new titles on a town wall with the bull's blood. While this is now "forbidden," and getting rare, some traditions refuse to die.

Salamanca Accommodations and Food

You may choose to stay overnight in Salamanca, giving you more time in Segovia and Salamanca and en route to Coimbra. (Tourist office tel. 218342.) In that case, try to stay on or near the Plaza Mayor. Prices vary from the cheap **Hostal Los Angeles** (Plaza Mayor 10, tel. 218166) to inexpensive pensions to expensive hotels with windows right on the square. The **Gran Hotel** (expensive, at Plaza Poeta Inglesias 6, just southeast of Plaza Mayor, tel. 213500) offers a luxurious splurge

There are plenty of good, inexpensive restaurants between the Plaza Mayor and the Gran Vía. Try **Las Torres** (Plaza Mayor 26), **Novelty** (Plaza Mayor, great coffee), **Mesón de Cervantes** (Plaza Mayor, good tapas, sit outside or upstairs), **La Covachuela** (Plaza Mercado 24), and several places on Calle Bermejeros (like **Taberna de Pilatos** and **De la Reina**). For a special dinner, go to **Chez Victor** (Espoz y Mina 22, closed Sundays and Mondays).

For nightlife, be chic at **Gatsby's** on Calle Bordaderos or enjoy jazz at **El Corillo** just southwest of the plaza.

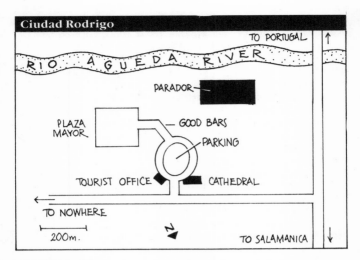

Ciudad Rodrigo
This beautiful old town of 16,000 people caps a hill overlooking
the Río Agueda. Spend an hour wandering among the Renaissance
mansions that line its streets and exploring the eighteenth-century
town walls. From these walls you can look into Portugal. The
castle is now a luxurious *parador* (a government-operated
hotel, often in a historic castle, always with a restaurant). A
budget way to enjoy the elegance is to splurge for a meal here.
Try coffee and tapas at **El Sanatorio** (Plaza Mayor 14) or any of
the busy bars between the plaza and the cathedral.

   Ciudad Rodrigo's cathedral has a special surprise. You'll see a
man outside a small door to the cloisters who, for a small price,
will take you on a walk through a series of twelfth-century
groin vaults ornamented with stone carvings racy enough to
make Hugh Hefner blush. Who said, "When you've seen one
Gothic church, you've see 'em all"?

Coimbra
Coimbra (pronounced KWEEM-bra) is a small town of winding
streets set on the side of a hill. The high point is the old university. From there, little lanes dribble down to Rua de Ferreira
Borges, the main business and shopping street, and the
Mondego River. The crowded, intense Old Quarter of town is
the triangle between the river and the Rua Ferreira Borges.
When school is in session, Coimbra bustles. During school holidays, it's sleepier.

   There are two train stations: A and B. Major trains all stop at B
(big). From there, it's easy to catch a small train to the very cen-

tral A station (just "take the A train"). The tourist office (Largo da Portagem, tel. 039/25576, open Monday-Saturday 9:00-20:00, Sunday 9:00-12:30, 14:00-18:00) and plenty of good budget rooms are near the A station (train information, tel. 34998).

From the Largo da Portagem (main square), everything is within an easy walk. The Old Quarter spreads out like an amphitheater—timeworn houses, shops, and stairways, all leading up to the old university.

The most direct route up the hill is to follow Rua Ferreira Borges away from the Largo da Portagem, then turn right under a twelfth-century arch (the marketplace is down the stairs to your left) and go up the steep alleyway called Rua de Quebra Costas—"Street of Broken Ribs"! From the old cathedral, turn right and circle around the old and new university buildings.

Accommodations
The more comfortable rooms lie on Avenida E. Navarro along the river. At **Hotel Astoria** (expensive, 21, tel. 22055), the rooms facing the hillside are quieter and have a fine city view. **Pensão Atlantico** (inexpensive, right behind Hotel Astoria at Rua Sargento Mar 42, tel. 26496) is much more reasonable. Cheaper and more interesting places are in the Old Quarter, especially on Rua da Sota, leaving Largo da Portagem to the west. There are plenty of $15-$20 doubles. Try **Pensão Rivoli** (inexpensive, Praça do Comercio 27, tel. 25550) or **Pensão Residencial Parque** (inexpensive, Avenida E. Navarro 42, tel. 29202, river view, English spoken). When all else fails, the "truck route" street, Avenida Fernando de Maghalaes, is lined with hotels.

Food
Most restaurants are near the river. There are a few local-style cafés near the old cathedral. I enjoy the stand-up bar **A Tasquinha** (Rua de Quebra Costas 56). **Restaurant Praça Velha** (Praça do Comercio 71, on the main square in the market-place) is a quiet break from the hectic Old Quarter. A good place for lunch (cheap, tasty, atmospheric but a bit seedy) is **Restaurant Alfredo** (cross the bridge, stay to the right, Avenida João das Negras 10). **Restaurant Funchal** (Rua das Azeiteiras 18) and **Churrasquería do Mondego** (Rua do Sargento 27, near Largo da Portagem) serve good, reasonably priced meals.

COIMBRA TO NAZARÉ

Today you'll tour the historic Coimbra University, then travel to the huge Gothic monastery at Batalha, finally arriving at your beach town headquarters on the Atlantic.

Suggested Schedule	
8:00	Breakfast in hotel or with busy locals in a bar on Rua Ferreira Borges.
8:30	Enjoy a shady morning in the Old Quarter alleys and shops. It's about a 15-minute walk to the university. Stop by the old cathedral on your way.
10:00	Tour Coimbra University.
12:00	Lunch.
13:30	Drive to Batalha. You'll pass the Roman ruins of Conimbriga and castles at Pombal and Leiria—none of great importance but each interesting to some.
15:30	Batalha Church (Monastery of Santa Maria).
17:30	Drive to Nazaré.

Coimbra
Don't be fooled by the ugly suburbs and monotonous concrete apartment buildings that surround the town. Portugal's most important city for 200 years, Coimbra remains second only to Lisbon culturally and historically. It was the center of Portugal while the Moors still controlled Lisbon. Only as Portugal's maritime fortunes rose was Coimbra surpassed by the port towns of Lisbon and Porto. Today Coimbra is Portugal's third largest city (pop. 70,000). It has its oldest and most prestigious university (founded 1307) and a great old quarter, with the flavor of a Moroccan Kasbah. The view from the south end of Santa Clara Bridge is a good introduction to Coimbra.

Sightseeing Highlights
Old Cathedral (Se Velha)—This dinky Romanesque church is built like a bulky but compact fortress, complete with crenellations. There's an interesting Flamboyant Gothic altarpiece inside. Open 10:00-12:30 and 14:00-17:00.
  ▲ **Old University**—Coimbra's 700-year-old university was modeled after the Bologna university (Europe's first, A.D. 1139).

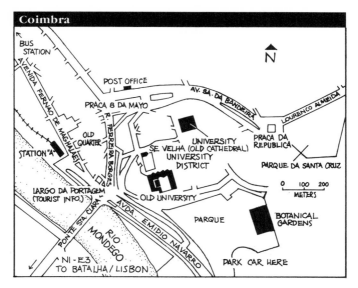

It's a stately, three-winged building, beautifully situated over-looking the city. At first, law, medicine, grammar, and logic were taught. Then, with Portugal's seafaring orientation, astronomy and geometry were added. The rich library has thousands of old books and historical documents surrounded by gilded ceil-ings and Baroque halls. The inlaid rosewood reading tables and the shelves of precious woods are a reminder that Portugal's wealth was great and imported. Enjoy the panoramic view and imagine being a student in Coimbra 500 years ago. Don't miss the Manueline-style chapel with its elaborate outside doors and lavish organ loft. Open 9:00-12:30 and 14:00-17:00; ring the doorbell to get in.

Old Quarter—If you can't make it to Morocco, this is the next best thing. For a breather from this intense shopping and sight-seeing experience, surface on the spacious Praça do Comercio for coffee or a beer (*cerveja*).

Conimbriga Roman Ruins—Not much of this Roman city has survived the ravages of time and barbarians. Still, there are some good floor mosaics and a museum. (Seven miles south of Coim-bra on N1, turn left to Condeixa. Open 9:00-13:00 and 14:00-20:00; museum closed Mondays.)

Transportation: Coimbra to Batalha to Nazaré (60 miles)
By car, you'll travel to Batalha on highway N1 (also called E3) for 90 minutes. From Batalha, it's a pleasant drive down N356, then N242 into Nazaré.

The train goes seven times daily from Coimbra to Nazaré with a change in Figueira da Foz. Batalha is better reached by bus. You'll go to Leiria first (2 hours) and catch one of eight daily buses from there to Alcobaca, via Batalha. From Batalha to Nazaré requires a change in Alcobaca.

Batalha: The Monastery of Santa María
This is Portugal's greatest architectural achievement and a symbol of its national pride. Batalha (which means "battle") was begun in 1388 to thank God for a Portuguese victory that kept her free from Spanish rule. The greatness of Portugal's Age of Discovery shines brightly in the Royal Cloisters, which combine the sensibility of Gothic with the elaborate decoration of the fancier Manueline style, and in the Chapter House with its frighteningly broad vaults. This heavy ceiling was considered so dangerous to build (it collapsed twice) that only prisoners condemned to death were allowed to work on it. Today it's considered stable enough to be the home of the Portuguese tomb of the unknown soldier. Also visit the Founder's Chapel with many royal tombs, including Henry the Navigator's. (Henry's the one wearing a church on his head.) The Batalha Abbey is great—but nothing else at this stop is. See it, then head for the coast. Open 9:00-18:00 daily.

Fatima
On May 13, 1917, the Virgin Mary visited three young shepherds and told them peace was needed. World War I raged on, so on the 13th of each of the next five months, Mary dropped in again to call for peace. Now, on the 13th of each month, thousands of pilgrims gather at the huge Neoclassical basilica of Fatima.
Fatima welcomes guests. It is an easy and interesting side trip (though not so easy around the 13th) just 12 miles east of Batalha.

Nazaré
In the summer, it seems that most of this famous town's 10,000 inhabitants are in the tourist trade. Nazaré is a hit with tour groups and masses of Lisbon day-trippers who come up to see traditionally clad fishermen do everything as traditionally as possible. The beach promenade is a congested tangle of oily sunbathers, hustlers, plastic souvenirs, overpriced restaurants, and, until they built the new harbor, romantic fishing boats.
Off-season, however, Nazaré is almost empty of tourists—inexpensive, colorful and relaxed.
Any time of year, even with its crowds, Nazaré is a fun stop offering a surprisingly good look at traditional Portugal. Prowl the beach, ride the funicular to the whitewashed old clifftop vil-

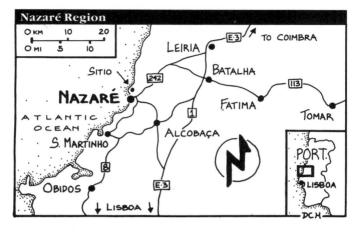

lage, the Sitio, for a staggering coastal view. Check out the traditional outfits the locals still wear. Be on the beach when the
fishing boats come in about 20:00.

Nazaré faces its long beach, stretching from its new harbor
north to the hill-capping old town, the Sitio. Your best home
base is the town center directly below the Sitio. The tourist
office is just off the beach on Avenida da República (tel. 52194;
open daily 10:00-22:00).

Accommodations
You should have no problem finding a room except in August,
when the crowds, temperature, and prices are all at their
highest. You'll find plenty of hustlers meeting each bus and
along the promenade. There are lots of *quartos* (rooms in private homes) and cheap, dingy pensions. I like to stay in the center near the water. Prices are higher, but it's worthwhile.

Ribamir Hotel Restaurant (expensive, Praça Sousa Oliveira
67-A, tel. 061/51158) has a prime location on the waterfront,
with an Old World, classy, well-worn, musty atmosphere,
including dark wood and four-poster beds; very hotellike.

Mar Bravo Pensão is on the corner where the main square
meets the waterfront next to Ribamir. Though it has less character, it's more modern, bright, and fresh, with a good restaurant
downstairs (moderate, Praça Sousa Oliviera 67-A, tel.
061/51180).

Residencial Marina (inexpensive, Rua Mouzinho de Albu-
querque 6-A, second floor, tel. 061/51541) is two blocks off the
waterfront on the central square. This place is old, clean, basic,
and quiet.

Residencial A Cubata (moderate, Avenida da República 6, tel. 062/51706) is a friendly place on the waterfront above the Bingo sign on the north end.

To avoid the crowds and enjoy a quiet piece of beach, stay in a small village eight miles south—São Martinho do Porto (pronounced "sow marteen yo"). There's tourist information right on the beach promenade in the São Martinho town center. The quaint old **Hotel Parque** (moderate, Avenida Marchal Carmona near the post office, tel. 98505), with its stucco ceilings and a peaceful park, is a good value.

There are several cheaper pensions nearby. The high-rise hotel (moderate) behind the Hotel Parque is a cheaper modern alternative, full of vacationing Germans. Or try the more atmospheric **Pensão Luz** up the hill from the center of town (inexpensive, tel. 98139).

There's a fine youth hostel, **Pousada de Juventude**, on a hill nearby above the village of Alfeizerão near São Martinho (tel. 99506).

Food

Nazaré is a fishing town, so don't order hamburgers. Fresh seafood is great all over town: more expensive (but affordable) along the waterfront, cheap in holes-in-walls farther inland. In Sitio, eat at **Marisqueira Paulo Caetano Restaurant** between the funicular and the square on the left. For informal fun, eat in the simple section, not the classy one. Try the local drinks— Amendoa Amarga (like Amaretto) and Licor Beirão.

BEACH DAY IN NAZARÉ, ALCOBACA SIDE TRIP

After all the traveling you've done, it's time for an easy day and some fun in the sun. Between two nights in your beach town, take a quick trip inland, spend the afternoon soaking up the sun, and savor an evening in a relaxed fishing village.

Suggested Schedule	
8:00	Breakfast at hotel.
8.30	Drive through countryside, visiting the wine museum, Alcobaca (town and monastery), and São Martinho do Porto.
13:00	Lunch back in Nazaré, ride the funicular up to Sitio, free time on beaches.
19:00	Seafood dinner—shrimp and *vinho verde*. Watch the boats come in as the shells pile up and the sun sets.

Circular Excursion through the Countryside (30 miles)
Leaving Nazaré, you'll pass women wearing the traditional seven petticoats as they do laundry at the edge of town on the road to Alcobaca. Within a few minutes you'll be surrounded by eucalyptus groves in a world that smells like a coughdrop. Then you land in Alcobaca, famous for its church, the biggest in Portugal and well worth a visit. The helpful tourist office is across the square from the church. Alcobaca's market will always shine brightly in my memory. It houses the Old World happily under its huge steel and glass dome. Inside, black-clad, dried-apple-faced women choose fish, chicks, birds, and rabbits from their respective death rows. You'll also find figs, melons, bushels of grain, and nuts—it's a caveman's Safeway. Buying a picnic is a perfect excuse to take a ride on this magic market carpet.

A half mile outside of town (on the road to Batalha and Leiria, right-hand side) you'll find the local cooperative winery, which runs the National Museum of Wine, a fascinating look at the wine of Portugal (9:00-12:00 and 14:00-17:00, closed Sundays). The tour, much more "hands-on" than French winery tours, is a walk through mountains of centrifuged, strained, and drained grapes—all well on the road to fermentation. The tour climaxes with a climb to the top of one of twenty half-buried 80,000-gallon tanks—all busy fermenting. Look out! I stuck my head into the manhole-sized top vent, and just as I focused on the rich, bubbling grape stew, I was walloped silly by a wine vapor-punch.

Return via the tiny fishing village of São Martinho do Porto. Back in Nazaré, you'll be greeted by the energetic applause of the forever surf and big plates of smiling steamed shrimp.

Nazaré doesn't have any blockbuster sights. The colorful fish market (Mercado de Peixe) near the beach on the south edge of town, dogs engaging in public displays of affection on the beach, and the funicular ride up to Sitio for some shopping and a great coastal view, along with the "sightseeing" my taste buds did, are the highlights of my lazy Nazaré memories. Plan for some good beach time here. Ask at the tourist office about bull-fights in the Sitio (most summer weekends) and folk dancing at the casino (two nights a week).

NAZARÉ, OBIDOS, AND LISBON

Today you'll travel just 60 miles, leaving the beach village to spend a few hours in Portugal's cutest walled city and then driving into Lisbon, where you'll set up for three nights.

Suggested Schedule	
9:00	Leave Nazaré.
10:00	Explore Obidos.
12:00	Drive into Lisbon, set up, visit tourist office.
14:00	Lunch on Rua das Portas de Santo Antão, stroll Avenida de Liberdade, explore downtown Rossio and Baixa center, shop.
18:00	Evening and dinner at Feira Popular.
Note:	Thursdays or Sundays: bullfights at 22:00 near Feira Popular.

Transportation: Nazaré to Obidos to Lisbon (60 miles)
Drivers will follow N242 south from Nazaré, passing São Martinho and its unique and inviting saltwater lake, and catch scenic N8 farther south to Obidos. Don't even think about driving in tiny, cobbled Obidos. Ample tourist parking is provided outside of town. From Obidos, take the no-nonsense direct route N115, N1, and E3 into Lisbon.

Driving in Lisbon is big-city crazy. Consider hiring a taxi (cheap) to lead you to your hotel. If you don't pay him until the mission is complete, he won't lose you. Ask at your hotel about safe parking in a city whose parking lots glitter with the crumbled remains of wing windows.

Public transportation becomes more regular as you approach Lisbon. Trains and buses go almost hourly from Nazaré through Obidos to Lisbon.

Both Nazaré and São Martinho are on the main Lisbon-Porto train line. The Nazaré station is three miles out of town near Valado (easy bus connection), and São Martinho's is about one mile from town. There are several buses a day from both towns to Batalha/Coimbra and to Lisbon via Obidos/Torres Vedras.

Obidos
This medieval walled town was Portugal's "wedding city"—the perfect gift for kings to give their queens. Today it is preserved in its entirety as a national monument, surviving on tourism. Obidos is crowded in July and August. Filter out the tourists and it's still great.

This postcard town sits atop a hill, its perfect 40-foot-high wall corraling a bouquet of narrow lanes and flower-decked, whitewashed houses. Walk around the wall, peek into the castle (now a lavish pousada—tel. 95105), lose yourself for a while in this lived-in open air museum of medieval city planning. It's fun to wander the back lanes, study the solid centuries-old houses, and think about progress. There's a small museum, an interesting Renaissance church with lovely azulejo walls inside, and, outside the walls, an aqueduct, a windmill, and a bustling market.

Obidos is tough on the budget. Pick up a picnic at the grocery store near the main gate. If you have time to spend the night, you'll enjoy the town without tourists. If you decide to sleep in Obidos, two good values in this overpriced touristic toy of a town are Casa do Poco (moderate, with shower, no breakfast, in the old center near the castle, tel. 95358), and the Estalagem do Convente (moderate, Rua Dr. João de Orvelas, just outside the old quarter, tel. 95217). For cheap intimacy, ask around for quartos (bed and breakfasts). The Obidos tourist office is open from 9:30 to 20:00 (tel. 062/95231). Pick up their handy town map listing bed and breakfast places.

A Side Trip to Seafood Paradise
When seafood lovers die, they bury their tongues in an otherwise uninteresting town called Ericeira. Just a few miles west from Torres Vedras, this place is a great lunch stop. Dozens of bars and restaurants pull the finest lobster, giant crab, mussels, and fish out of the sea and serve them up fresh and cheap. Six dollars will buy you a meal fit for Neptune. Most places are on the main street.

There are good beaches just a few miles north and south of Ericeira. Buses run several times daily between Lisbon, Sintra, and Ericeira.

Lisbon
Lisbon is easy. The city center is in a valley flanked by two hills. In the middle of the valley is Rossio Square, the heart of Lisbon, with plenty of buses, subways, and cheap taxis leaving in all directions. Between the Rossio and the harbor is the lower city, Baixa, with its checkerboard street plan, elegant architecture, bustling shops and many cafés. Most of Lisbon's prime attractions are within walking distance of the Rossio.

On a hill to the west of the Rossio is the old and noble shopping district of Chiado. Above that is the Baírro Alto (upper quarter) with its dark bars, hidden restaurants, and many fado places.

East of the Rossio is another hill blanketed by the medieval

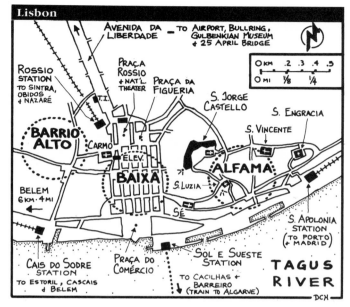

Alfama quarter and capped by the Castelo São Jorge. Avenida Liberdade is the tree-lined "Champs Elysées" of Lisbon, connecting the old lower town with the newer upper end.

The main tourist information office is at the lower end of Avenida Liberdade in the Palacio da Foz at Praça dos Restauradores, just north of Rossio (Monday-Saturday 9:00-20:00, Sundays 10:00-18:00, tel. 363643; 24-hour telephone service, 893689). It's friendly and helpful. I even got help pronouncing my basic Portugese phrases. There are also offices at Castelo São Jorge, at Miradouro da Santa Luzia above the Alfama, in the Apolonia station and at the airport.

Banks, the post office, airlines, and travel agents line the Avenida Liberdade. American Express is in the Star Travel Agency (tel. 539871, open Monday-Friday 9:00-12:30 and 14:00-18:00, helpful, offering clients mail service), at Avenida Sidonio País 4A, and at Praça dos Restauradores 14.

Lisbon has four train stations (see map). Santa Apolonia is the major station, handling all international trains and trains that go to north and east Portugal. It's just past the Alfama, with good bus connections to the town center (bus 9 goes from Santa Apolonia Station through the center and up Avenida Liberdade), tourist information, a room-finding service, and 24-hour currency exchange service. Barreiro Station, a 30-minute ferry ride across the Tagus River from Praça do Comercio, is for trains to the Algarve and points south. Rossio Station goes to Sintra and the west), and Caís do Sodre Station handles the 30-minute rides to Cascais and Estoril.

The airport, just five miles northeast of downtown, has good bus connections to town, cheap taxis, a 24-hour bank, tourist office, and a guarded parking lot ($4.00/day, tel. 802060).

Lisbon has fine public transportation. Park your car in a guarded lot and use taxis and buses. The very central Praça do Comercio at the water's edge has a large pay lot, which may be your best temporary stop until you locate a hotel.

Tourists' cars are unsafe overnight downtown. There are several guarded lots (get advice from your hotel), or park your car at the airport. You'll see it on the main road at the north end of town.

The Lisbon subway is simple, clean, fast, and cheap but runs only north of the Rossio into the new town. It runs from 6:00 to 1:00. The big letter "M" marks metro stops. The bus system is great. Pick up the "Guía dos Transportes Públicos de Lisboa e Região" for specifics on buses in and around Lisbon. Lisbon's colorful vintage trolley system is San Francisco fun. Line #28 from Graca to Prazeres offers a great Lisbon joy ride. Pick it up at Rua da Conceicão in Baixa. (It goes to Chiado and Santa Clara near the flea market and Alfama.)

Lisbon taxis are cheap (50 cents drop charge plus 50 cents a mile) and abundant. I taxi here more than anywhere else in Europe.

Thieves abound in Lisbon. Be on a theft alert everywhere, but particularly in the Alfama, Baírro Alto, and anywhere at night.

Accommodations

Finding a room in Lisbon is easy. Cheap and charming ride the same teeter-totter, so the price you choose will generally determine the mix you get. If you arrive late, or in August, the room-finding services in the station and at the airport are very helpful. Most of my listings fill up every night in August, so call ahead. Otherwise, just wander through the district of your choice and find your own bed. If you have a room reserved, take the taxi from the station—it's only a dollar or two.

Many pensions ($15-$25 doubles) are around the Rossio and in the side streets near the Avenida Liberdade. Quieter and more colorful places are in the Baírro Alto and around the Castle São Jorge, though those areas are a little sleazy at night.

Downtown (Baixa and Rossio Area): This area is as central, safe, and bustling as possible in Lisbon, with lots of shops, traffic, people, and urban intensity. **Residencia Campos** (inexpensive, Rua Jardim do Regedor 24, third floor, tel. 320560) is very friendly, clean, and simple, with a perfect location just off Praça dos Restauradores across from the tourist office; some English spoken. **Hotel Avenida Palace** (very expensive, Rua 1 de Dezembro 123, tel. 360151), a huge, well-worn piece of the Old World, has crystal chandeliers and heavy furniture, lots of uniformed service, a very central location on Praça dos Restauradores and will hold a room if you telephone. **Pensão Norte** (inexpensive, Rua dos Douradores 159, just off Praça da Figueira and Rossio, tel. 878941) is very central, plain, and clean, but they speak no English. **Hotel Suisso Atlantico** (moderate, Rua da Gloria 3-19, just behind the funicular station at Praça dos Restauradores, tel. 361713) has a perfect location. It's formal, hotelish, and a bit stuffy, with lots of tour groups, but has great rooms and a lounge that make it a wonderful value.

Chiado and Baírro Alto: Just west of downtown, this area is more colorful, has less traffic, and is a bit seedy, but it's full of ambience, good bars, and markets. This area may not feel comfortable for women alone at night. **Hotel Borges** (moderate, Rua Garrett 108, on the shopping street next to A Braziliera café, tel. 361951) is a fine Old World hotel splurge. **Residencial Camões** (inexpensive, Trav. Poco da Cidade 38, tel. 367510) lies right in the seedy thick of the Baírro Alto but maintains a bright, cheery, and very safe feeling. It's friendly, with great rooms and English spoken.

Pensão Duque (cheap, Calçada do Duque 53, tel. 363444) has a great location on the pedestrian stairway street just off Largo Trinidad at the edge of Baírro Alto, up from Rossio. English is spoken by a friendly staff. This place is too seedy for most, though, with an ancient tangle of steep stairways, tacky vinyl floors and droopy beds. The price, location, and saggy ancient atmosphere make it a prize for some, but water and just about everything else are down the hall.

Residencial Nova Silva (inexpensive, Rua Victor Cordón 11, tel. 324371) has a fine location between Baírro Alto and the river, providing some great river views. The owner, English-speaking Mehdi Kara, is friendly and very helpful. The place is a bit shabby, but that's Lisbon. It's often full, so call well in advance and reconfirm two days early. Rooms with a view are given to those who stay longest, but ask anyway.

Uptown: Residencia Caravela (moderate, Rua Ferreira Lapa 38, next to Avenida Duque de Loule, tel. 539011) doesn't have much character and isn't so central (near Parque Eduardo VII), but it's clean, practical, friendly, and English-speaking. Nearby and about the same is **Residencia Norea Castanheirense** (Rua Gomes Freire 130, tel. 528617).

York House, also called **Residencia Inglesa** (expensive, Rua Janeles Verdes 32, tel. 662435), is popular for its pleasant

English atmosphere in an old villa with a garden out toward Belem district.

Lisbon's **Pousada de Juventude (Youth Hostel)** is central, cheap, and decent, closed from 10:30 to 18:00 daily, it is at Rua Andrade Corvo 46, near American Express (bus #44 or #45, tel. 532696).

When searching for a pension, remember: singles are a lot more expensive per person than doubles; a building may contain several different pensions; addresses like 26-3° mean street 26, third floor (which is fourth floor in American terms).

To enjoy a more peaceful, old beach resort atmosphere away from the big-city intensity, establish headquarters at Cascais, just 14 miles away. Cheap, 30-minute trains go downtown several times an hour.

Food

The smaller pensions actually serve breakfast in bed since they have no dining area. Or try one of the traditional coffeehouses, like the bustling **Café Suiza** on the Rossio.

Memorable pastry and delicious hot chocolate are at Ferrari (Rua Nova do Almada 93). The world's greatest selection of port wines is nearby at **Solar do Vinho do Porto**, Rua São Pedro de Alcantara 45. For a small price, you can taste any of 250 different ports, though you may want to try only 125 on one night and save the rest for the next night.

Lisbon has several great restaurant districts.

Alfama: This gritty chunk of preearthquake Lisbon is full of interesting eateries, especially along the Rua San Pedro (the main drag) and on Largo de São Miguel. For a colorful lunch after your Alfama exploration, eat at **Restaurante Farol de Santa Luzia** (Largo de Santa Luzia 5, across from the tiled patio viewpoint overlooking the Alfama called Miradouro de Santa Luzia, just below the castle, overlooking the Alfama). A good splurge in this area, with a harbor view, is the **Faz O Figura** at Rua do Paraíso 15B (expensive, call 868-981 for reservations).

While in the Alfama, be sure to drop into a few dark bars. Have an aperitif, taste the *blanco seco* (local dry wine). Make a friend, pet a chicken, read the graffiti, pick at the humanity ground between the cobbles.

Baírro Alto: Lisbon's "old town" is full of small, fun, and cheap places. Fisherman's bars line the Rua Nova Trinidade. Deeper into the Baírro Alto, past Rua Misericordia, you'll find the area's best meals. The **Cervejaría da Trinidade** at Rua Nova da Trinidade 20C (tel. 323506, closed Wednesdays) is a Portuguese-style beer hall, covered with great tiled walls and full of fish and locals. You'll remember a dinner here.

Between Chiado and the river (next to recommended

Residencial Nova Silva), just off Rua Victor Cordón at Travessa do Ferragial 1, is a colorful self-service restaurant run by the Catholic Church, with a very local feel, great food, impossibly cheap prices, and riverview terrace. Open 12:00-15:00, closed August.

Coffeehouse aficionados should not miss Lisbon's grand old café, **A Brasiliera** at Rua Garret 122. A very lively place to eat is **Galeto** on Avenida da República 14.

The "eating lane"—Rua das Portas de Santo Antão—just east of Praça dos Restauradores, is a galloping gourmet's heaven with a galaxy of eateries to choose from. The seafood is Lisbon's best. Rather than siesta, have a small black coffee (called a *bica*) in a shady café on the Avenida Liberdade.

Back near Praça dos Restauradores behind Rossio Square, consider the restaurant at Rua dos Condotles 29-35 (clean, popular with locals, fresh seafood, good value). In the suburb of Belem, you'll find several good restaurants along Rua de Belem between the coach museum and the monastery.

O Policia, Rua Marquesa da Bandeira 112 (an easy taxi ride from the center, just behind the Gulbenkian Museum, tel. 763505) has great local food (the best meal I've had in Portugal), an interesting scene, and very good service by an entire academy of cute cops (at least they look like cops). Open Monday-Friday 12:00-15:00, 19:00-22:00, Saturday 12:00-16:00, moderate prices.

Finally, don't miss a chance to go purely local with hundreds of Portuguese families having salad, fries, chicken, and wine at the Feira Popular. More on eating is built into the sample schedules.

LISBON

Plunge into the Lisbon jungle, touring its salty sailors' quarter, exploring its hill-capping castle, enjoying its top art gallery, and eating, sipping, and browsing your way through its colorful shopping districts. Wrap up the day atmospherically with seafood and folk music.

Suggested Schedule

8:00	Breakfast.
9:00	Tour castle São Jorge. Meander through the Alfama from Miradour de Santa Luzia.
12:00	Lunch in Alfama or at O Policio near museum.
14:00	Tour Gulbenkian Art Museum.
15:30	Taxi to Chiado, shop along Rua Garrett, have coffee at A Brasiliera, explore Baírro Alto, view the city from San Pedro Terrace. Ride the funicular back downtown.
18:30	Relax at hotel.
20:00	Taxi to Cervejaría da Trinidade for dinner or go to a dinner fado show in the Baírro Alto neighborhood.

Lisbon
Lisbon is a wonderful mix of now and then. Old wooden trolleys shiver up and down its hills, bird-stained statues mark grand squares, taxis rattle and screech through cobbled lanes, and well-worn people sip coffee in art nouveau cafés.

Present-day Lisbon is explained by her past. While her history goes back to Roman and Moorish days, her glory days were the fifteenth and sixteenth centuries when explorers like Vasco da Gama opened up new trade routes and made Lisbon Europe's richest city. The economic boom brought the flamboyant art boom called the Manueline period. Later, in the early eighteenth century, the riches of Brazil made Lisbon even wealthier. Then in 1755, a tremendous earthquake leveled the city, killing over 20 percent of its population.

Lisbon was rebuilt under the energetic, and eventually dictatorial, leadership of the Marquis Pombal. The charm of preearthquake Lisbon survives only in Belem, the Alfama, and the Baírro Alto district. The Pombal-designed downtown is on a strict grid plan, symmetrical, with broad boulevards and square squares.

While the earthquake flattened a lot of buildings, its colonial empire is long gone, and a 1988 fire destroyed another chunk of her old town, Lisbon's heritage is alive and well. Barely elegant outdoor cafés, exciting art, bustling bookstores, entertaining museums, the saltiest sailors' quarter in Europe, and much more, all at bargain basement prices, make Lisbon an Iberian highlight.

Sightseeing Highlights

▲▲▲ **Alfama**—This most colorful sailors' quarter in Europe was the Visigothic birthplace of Lisbon, a rich district during the Arabic period, and then the home of Lisbon's fisherfolk. One of the few areas to survive the 1755 earthquake, the Alfama is a cobbled cornucopia of Old World color. A visit is best during the busy midmorning market time (10:00) or in the late afternoon/early evening when the streets teem with locals.

Wander deep. This urban jungle's roads are squeezed into tangled and confused alleys; bent houses comfort each other in their romantic shabbiness, and the air drips with laundry and the smell of clams and raw fish. You'll probably get lost, but that doesn't matter unless you're trying to stay found. Poke aimlessly, sample ample grapes, avoid rabid-looking dogs, peek through windows.

Electrico streetcars #10, #11, and #26 go to the Alfama. On Tuesdays and Saturdays, the Feira da Ladra flea market rages on the nearby Campo de Santa Clara (bus #12, trolley #28).

▲ **Castelo São Jorge**—The city castle, with a history going back to Roman days, caps the hill above the Alfama and offers a pleasant garden and the finest view of Lisbon. Use this perch to orient yourself. Open daily until sunset.

▲ **Fado**—Mournfully beautiful, haunting ballads about lost sailors, broken hearts, and sad romance are one of Lisbon's favorite late-night pastimes. Be careful, this is also one of those cultural clichés that all too often become tourist traps. The Alfama has many fado bars, but most are terribly touristy. The Baírro Alto is your best bet. Things don't start until 22:00 and then take an hour or two to warm up. A fado performance isn't cheap (expect a $10 cover), and many fado joints require dinner. Ask at your hotel for advice. I've found dinner shows to be the best value.

▲▲ **Gulbenkian Museum**—This is easily the best of Lisbon's forty museums. Gulbenkian, an Armenian oil tycoon, gave his art collection (or "harem," as he called it) to Portugal in gratitude for the hospitable asylum granted him there during WWII. Now this great collection spanning 2,000 years of art is displayed in a classy and comfortable modern building.

Visit the great Egyptian and Greek sections and the few
masterpieces by Rembrandt, Rubens, Renoir, Rodin, and artists
whose names start with other letters. There's a good, cheap, air-
conditioned cafeteria and nice gardens. Take bus line #15, #30,
#31, #41, #46 or #56 from downtown, or Sete-Ríos metro line to
the "Palhava" stop, or pay 200 escudos for a taxi from Rossio.
Open Tuesday, Thursday, Friday, Sunday 10:00-17:00; Wednesday and Saturday 14:00-19:30 in summer; closed Mondays.
Admission is 40 escudos.

Museum Nacional de Arte Antigua—Here you can see paintings and rich furniture from the days when Portugal owned the
world. (Rua das Janeles Verdes 9, open 10:00-13:00 and 14:30-
17:00; closed Mondays.)

▲▲▲ **Bullfights**—The Portuguese *tourada* could be considered a humane version of the Spanish *corrida*—the Portugese
don't kill the bull. After an equestrian prelude, a colorfully clad,
eight-man team enters the ring. The leader prompts the bull to
charge, and he sprints into the bull, meeting him right between
the padded horns. As he hangs onto the bull's head, his buddies
then pile on, trying to wrestle it to a standstill. Finally, one guy
hangs on to el toro's tail and water-skis behind him. The season
lasts from April through October, and you're most likely to see a
fight in Lisbon, Estoril, or on the Algarve. Fights start late in the
evening. Get schedules at the tourist office. In Lisbon, there are
fights at Capo Pequeno every Thursday and many Sundays at
22:00. Tickets are available at the door or from the kiosk across
from the central tourist office.

▲▲▲ **Feira Popular (The People's Fair)**—By all means
spend an evening at Lisbon's Feira Popular, which rages nightly
May 1 to September 30 from 19:00 to midnight, Saturdays and
Sundays 15:00 to midnight. Located on Avenida da República at
the "Entre-Campos" metro stop, this fair bustles with Portuguese families at play. Pay the tiny entry fee, then enjoy rides,
munchies, great people-watching, entertainment, music—basic
Portuguese fun. Have dinner here among chattering families,
with endless food and wine paraded frantically in every direction. Wine stalls dispense wine from the udders of porcelain
cows. Fried ducks drip, barbecues spit, and dogs squirt the legs
of chairs while, somehow, local lovers ignore everything but
each other's eyes.

▲ **Cristo Rei**—A huge statue of Christ (a la Rio de Janeiro)
overlooks Lisbon from across the Tagus River. A lift takes you to
the top, and the view is worth the effort. Boats leave from
downtown constantly (buses connect every 20 minutes). A taxi
will charge you round-trip, but it's exciting to get the ride over
Lisbon's great 25th of April suspension bridge (Europe's largest).
Open 10:00-18:00 daily.

Best city views—The Castelo São Jorge offers the best view of Lisbon and a great way to get oriented. The other most impressive views are from Cristo Rei and along the São Pedro Terrace in the Baírro Alto (up Rua do Misericordia).

Shopping—Lisbon is Europe's bargain basement. You'll find decaying, but still elegant, department stores, teeming flea markets, and classy specialty shops. The Mercado Ribeira open-air market, next to the Cais do Sodre market, bustles every morning except Sunday—great for picnic stuff and local sweaters. Look for shoes, bags, and leather goods on Rua Garrett and Rua Carmo and gold and silver on the Rua do Ouro (Gold Street). Stores are furnished like museums—the palatial, but run-down, Grandes Armazenas do Chiado (Rua do Carmo 2) in its day was the Portuguese answer to London's Harrod's.

SINTRA AND THE ATLANTIC COAST

Recall Portugal's seafaring glory days with a morning in the sub-urb of Belem; then spend the afternoon climbing through the Versailles of Portugal, a windy, desolate, and ruined Moorish castle, and exploring the rugged and picturesque westernmost tip of Portugal. Mix and mingle with the jet set (or at least peek through their windows) at the resort towns of Cascais or Estoril before returning to Lisbon.

Suggested Schedule

8:00	Breakfast, buy picnic lunch.
9:00	Drive to Belem.
10:00	Tour Belem to see the glories of Lisbon's Golden Age. Picnic at Belem Tower or lunch on Rua de Belem.
14:00	Drive to Sintra, tour Pena Palace, explore the Moorish ruined castle (great picnic spot if you rush Belem). Possibly look at the lush garden of Monserrate.
17:00	Drive out to Capo da Roca.
18:00	Evening in resort of Estoril or Cascais.

Transportation: Circular Excursion, Lisbon to Sintra to Capo da Roca to Cascais to Lisbon (about 40 miles)
This trip is easy and most fun by car, and it might be a day when even bus and train travelers would enjoy a rental car. You'll find several companies on Avenida Liberdade.

Public transportation is workable. Trains go from Lisbon to Sintra (50 minutes) and Cascais (30 minutes) three times an hour, and buses connect points farther west. Buses connect Sintra, Capo da Roca, and Cascais. With some help from the tourist office, you can manage this circle fine on public transportation.

Belem
The Belem District, three miles from downtown Lisbon, is a pincushion of important sights from Portugal's Golden Age, when Vasco da Gama and company made her Europe's richest power. You can get there by bus (#12, #29, #43), by fun, old, very cheap streetcars (#15, #16, #17 from Praça do Comercio; wave to stop them, enter at the rear, and ring the stop bell by pulling the tether), or by taxi.

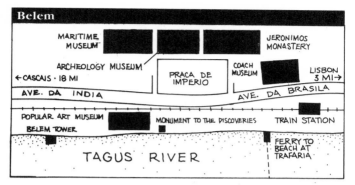

The Belem Tower, the only purely Manueline building in Portugal (built 1515), protected Lisbon's harbor and today symbolizes the voyages that made her powerful. This was the last sight sailors saw as they left and the first one they'd see when they returned loaded down with gold, diamonds, social diseases, and spices. (Open Tuesday-Sunday 9:00-18:00.) It's bare on the inside and not worth the admission to climb for the view.

The giant Monument to the Discoveries was built in 1960 to honor Henry the Navigator, who died 500 years earlier. Huge statues of Henry and Portugal's leading explorers line the giant concrete prow. Note the marble map chronicling Portugal's expansion on the ground in front. Inside you can take a lift for a view.

The Monastery of Jeronimos is possibly Portugal's most exciting building. In the giant church and its cloisters, notice how nicely the Manueline style combines Gothic and Renaissance features with motifs from the sea—the source of wealth that made this art possible. Don't miss the elegant cloisters—my favorite in Europe (open 10:00-18:30, closed Mondays, 150 escudos).

The Belem museums are somewhere between good and mediocre, depending on your interests. The coach museum has over 70 dazzling carriages from the eighteenth century (10:00-17:00, closed Mondays). The pop art museum takes you one province at a time through Portugal's folk art (10:00-12:30 and 14:00-17:00, closed Mondays). The maritime museum is a cut above the average European maritime museum. Sailors love it. Open 10:00-17:00, closed Mondays, 100 escudos.

Sintra
Just 12 miles north of Lisbon, Sintra was the summer escape of Portugal's kings. Byron called it a "glorious Eden." It's a lush playground of castles, palaces, sweeping coastal views, and

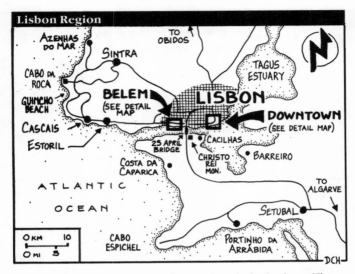

exotic gardens. You could easily spend a whole day here. The
tourist office on the town's main square is open daily (tel.
31157).

In the town, ten minutes from the train station, tour the
strange, but lavish, Palacio Nacional (10:00-17:00, closed Wednesdays). Then drive, climb (two miles), or taxi to the thousand-
year-old Moorish castle ruins (Castelo dos Mouros). Lost in an
enchanted forest and alive with winds of the past, these ruins
are a castle-lover's dream come true and a great place for a picnic with a panoramic Atlantic view.

Nearby is the magical hilltop Pena Palace (Palacio da Pena).
Portugal's German-born Prince Ferdinand hired a German
architect to build him a fantasy castle mixing elements of German and Portugese style. He got a crazy fortified salad of
Gothic, Arabic, Moorish, Walt Disney, Renaissance, and Manueline architectural bits and decorative pieces. The palace, built in
the 1840s, is preserved just as it was when the royal family fled
Portugal in 1910. For a spectacular view of Lisbon and the Tagus,
hike for 15 minutes from the palace to the chapel of Santa Eufe-
mia (you'll see signs). Open 10:00-17:00, closed Mondays.

Also in the area is the wonderful garden of Monserrate. If
you like tropical plants and exotic landscaping, this is definitely
for you.

Although nearly everyone who visits Sintra is day-tripping
from Lisbon, it's a fine place to spend a night. The Pensão Nova

Sintra (inexpensive, tel. 9230220) and the Estalagem da Raposa
are two of several good—and nostalgic—hotels. Colares, also
near Sintra, is another sleepy place with a salty breeze. You
could spend the night downtown at the Pensão Vareza (tel.
299-0008).

Capo da Roca
The wind-beaten Capo da Roca is the westernmost point in
Europe. It has a fun little shop, an information booth, and a
place where you can have a drink and pick up your "proof of
being here" diploma. Nearby, the Praia (beach) das Macas is a
good place for wind, waves, sand, and sun.

Cascais and Estoril
Before the rise of the Algarve, these towns were the haunt of
Portugal's rich and beautiful. Today, they are quietly elegant
with noble old buildings, beachfront promenades, a bullring,
and a casino. Cascais is the more enjoyable of the two, not as
rich and stuffy, with a cozy touch of fishing village, some
great seafood places, such as the Costa Azul (at Rua Sebastio Jose de
C. Melo 3), and a younger, less pretentious atmosphere.

For a Swim
The water at Cascais is filthy, and the Lisbon city beach at Costa
da Caparica is too crowded. For the best swimming around,
drive (public transportation is difficult) 30 miles south to the
golden beaches, shell-shaped bay, restaurants, and warm, clean
water at little Port Portinho da Arrabida. Or, better yet, wait for
the Algarve.

LISBON TO THE ALGARVE

Trade the big city for a sleepy fishing village on the south coast and a chance to enjoy Portugal's best beach. The route can be fast and direct, or you can detour inland to tour historic Évora and explore the Portuguese interior's dusty droves of olive groves and scruffy seas of cork trees on your way. The Algarve is the coast of any sun worshiper's dreams. It's so good, I'd get there pronto. Your Algarve hideaway and goal for the day is the fishing village of Salema.

Suggested Schedule	
9:00	Depart, drive over 25th of April Bridge.
10:00	Go to top of Cristo Rei for a great view of Lisbon.
11:00	Drive south to Salema.
16:00	Set up in Salema, dinner on beach.
Note:	Saturdays at 16:00—bullfights in Lagos.

Transportation: Lisbon to Salema (150 miles)
Drive south over Lisbon's 25th of April Bridge (Europe's longest suspension bridge, 1½ miles, built in 1966). A short detour just over the bridge takes you to the giant Christ in Majesty statue. Then continue south past Setubal and follow N120 to the south coast. For a short break and an interesting walk along some coastal sand dunes, stop at Costa de Santo Andre (just north of Sines). Just before Lagos, take the N268 road to Vila do Bispo and then east to Praia da Salema. The Algarve has good roads—and lots of traffic.

The Lisbon-Algarve (Lagos or Tavira) train (four departures daily) takes about six hours. The overnight train (arriving at 7:00) is a great way to maximize beach time and save money. Express buses are faster (four to six hours) but must be booked ahead of time (get details at the tourist office). Train service between the main towns along the south coast is excellent (nearly hourly between Lagos and the Spanish border). Buses will take you where the trains don't. Lagos is the nearest train station to Salema, a 15-mile hitch or bus ride away. (Ignore Lagos' "quartos women" who will tell you it's closer to 50 miles away.)

Évora and the Interior Option
With more time, you can visit Évora and Portugal's wild, but sleepy, interior. The villages you'll pass through in southern

Alentejo are poor, quiet, and, in many cases, dying. Unemployment here is so bad that many locals have left their hometowns for jobs—or the hope of jobs—in the big city. This is the land of the "black widows," women whose husbands have abandoned them to find work.

Évora

Évora has been a cultural oasis in the barren, arid plains of the southern province of Alentejo for 2,000 years. With a beautifully untouched provincial atmosphere, a fascinating whitewashed old quarter, plenty of museums, a cathedral, and even a Roman temple, Évora stands proud amid groves of cork and olive trees.

The major sights (Roman temple of Diana, early Gothic cathedral, archbishop's palace, and a luxurious pousada in a former monastery) crowd closely together at the town's highest point. Osteophiles eat up the macabre "House of Bones" chapel at the Church of St. Francis. It's lined with the bones of 5,000 monks. A subtler, but still powerful, charm is contained within the town's medieval wall. Find it by losing yourself in the quiet lanes of Évora's far corners.

The tourist offices are at Praça do Giraldo 73 (tel. 22671, open 9:00-19:00 Monday-Friday, a little less on weekends) and at the city entrance on the highway from Lisbon. For budget eating and sleeping, look around the central square, Praça do Giraldo. For a splurge, sleep in one of Portugal's most luxurious pousadas, the Convento dos Loios (across from the Roman temple, tel. 23079, expensive). I ate well for a moderate price at O Fialho (at Travessa Mascarhenas 14). For very local atmosphere, eat at the "Restaurant" restaurant just off the Praça at 11 Rua Romano Romalha.

From Évora, drivers head south to Beja, west to Aljustrel, then south by any number of equal routes. The fastest is to follow the signs southwest to Odemira, then turn south toward Albufeira. All the roads are a mix of straight and winding, well-paved and washboard, and you'll spend your share of time in third gear.

Beja, with its NATO base, is nothing special. Its castle has a military museum (open 10:00-13:00 and 14:00-18:00) and a territorial view, and the old town is worth a look and a cup of coffee.

A more enjoyable stop on your drive south would be for a refreshing swim in one of the lonely lakes of the Alentejo Desert, such as Baragem do Maranho or Baragem do Montargil.

Plan on arriving at the resort town of Lagos on the southern coast by 18:00. From here, drive west about halfway to Cape Sagres, then turn south down the small road to the humble beach town of Salema.

Accommodations

Lying where a dirt road hits the sea, Salema has three streets, a couple of hotels, a handful of restaurants, a private luxury condo-villa on the edge of town, and a lane full of fisherfolk who happily rent out rooms to foreign guests.

I'd skip the hotels and go for the quartos (bed-and-breakfast places). Just ask at the bar, or ask one of the friendly locals for a "room to let $6.50." There are plenty of private homes renting rooms along the town's residential street, which runs left from the village center as you face the beach. Prices vary dramatically with the season but are never expensive. Rooms usually have characteristic, but decent, plumbing, and many have beachfront balconies or views. Freddi or Martin at the **Louisa and Catarina Bar** can help you find a room. Few of the locals speak English, but they're used to dealing with visitors.

Restaurant Pensión Mare (Praia de Salema, Ville do Bispo 8650, Algarve—the little building with the flags on the hill just above the main road) is a careful and tidy paradise for British sunseekers, run by a British couple, Graham and Janet. Their moderately priced rooms are simple but good. All plumbing is down the hall. Guests must stay a minimum of three nights. They speak English better than I do and will hold rooms until 18:00 with a phone call (tel. 082/65165).

Private Rooms: The only sizable place on the "quartos street" is the brown tiled building on the left with **"Romen"** on the buzzer. The place is run by Romen Vlegas (eight inexpensive doubles, no English, tel. 65128). Their daughter speaks English, lives in Lisbon (tel. 2533375), and can arrange a room for you.

Campers sleep free and easy on the beach (public showers available in the town center) or can enjoy a fine new campground half a mile inland, back toward the main road.

Eating in Salema

Fresh seafood eternally. Salema has six or eight places to eat. The three that face the beach are the most fun with the best service, food, and atmosphere. The center beach bar **Atlantico** is my choice, especially the omelets for breakfast. The two-story **Bar Carioca** (with the parrot painted on the side), 30 yards off the beach, is the hip hangout. It has great pizza and fresh grilled fish served in a friendly atmosphere.

ALGARVE AND SAGRES

Today will be a day of rigorous rest and intensive relaxation on the beaches of Salema and in town, with a short side trip to explore the windy "land's end" of Portugal, Cape Sagres.

Suggested Schedule

Lazy Plan:

10:00	Breakfast at Sagres Pousada.
11:00	Explore Cape Sagres and Cape St. Vincent.
13:00	Lunch and afternoon on Salema beach seeing how slow you can get your pulse.

Or, for the Speedy Ones:

Morning	Breakfast at Sagres Pousada, explore Cape Sagres, Cape St. Vincent, and Beliche.
Lunch	On the west coast in the lovely town of Carrapateira.
Afternoon and Evening	In Lagos, the region's top resort town, with a possible bullfight and a visit to Praia da Roca near Portimão.

The Algarve

The Algarve, Portugal's southern coast, has long been known as Europe's last undiscovered tourist frontier. That statement, like "jumbo shrimp" and "military intelligence," contradicts itself. The Algarve is well discovered, and most of it is going the way of the Spanish Costa del Sol—paved, packed, and pretty stressful.

One bit of old Algarve magic still glitters quietly in the sun—Salema. You'll find it at the end of a small road just off the main drag between the big city of Lagos and the rugged "land's end" of Europe, Cape Sagres. This simple fishing village, quietly discovered by British and German tourists, is the best beach town left on the Algarve. It has a few hotels, time-share condos up the road, some "hippies," bars with rock music, English and German menus and signs (bullfight ads for "Stierkampf"), a lovely beach, and lots of sun. June through September, buses connect Lagos and Salema (five a day, under one hour).

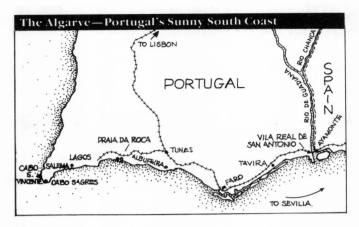

The Algarve — Portugal's Sunny South Coast

Cape Sagres
From Salema it's a short drive or hitch to the rugged and historic southwestern tip of Portugal. This was the spot closest to the edge of our flat earth in the days before Columbus. Prince Henry the Navigator, who was determined to broaden Europe's horizons, sent sailors ever farther into the unknown. He had a navigator's school at Cape Sagres. Henry carefully debriefed the many shipwrecked and frustrated explorers who washed ashore here.

Today, fishermen cast from its towering crags, local merchants sell seaworthy sweaters, and the windswept landscape harbors sleepy beaches, a salty village, and the lavish Pousada do Infante. For a touch of local elegance, pop by the pousada for breakfast.

Sagres is a popular gathering place for the backpacking crowd. The youth hostel is fun, comfortable, and historic (in the fort, tel. 64129), and there are plenty of private rooms available as well as some pleasant beaches. Buses connect Sagres and Lagos seven times daily.

Hints on Salema
Salema has a flatbed truck market that rolls in each morning— one truck for fruit, one for vegetables, and one for clothing and other odds and ends. A highlight of any Salema day is watching the fishing boats come and go (a tractor drags them in). Some bring in pottery jars that have sat on the ocean's bottom. Octopuses inhabit them and are hauled in—the last mistake they will ever make. Many of the quartos' landladies will happily clean your laundry for next to nothing. Salema is most crowded in July, August, and September.

ACROSS THE ALGARVE TO SEVILLA

After several days of storing up solar energy, it's time to hit the road again. You'll make a few short Algarve stops, then catch the tiny ferry to Spain and take the freeway into the flamenco city of Sevilla.

Suggested Schedule	
8:00	Depart Salema.
9:00	Breakfast and stroll through Lagos.
11:00	Drive to Tavira.
13:00	Lunch and browse in Tavira.
15:00	Drive to Sevilla (set clock ahead one hour).
18:00	Arrive in Sevilla. First stop: tourist office. Set up in hotel, dinner in Santa Cruz area.

Transportation: Algarve to Sevilla (150 miles)
Drive east along the Algarve. (If the traffic is bad, take the smaller N270 road to Tavira. It's a two- or three-hour drive from Salema to Tavira.) At Vila Real you'll catch the inexpensive 15-minute ferry ($4.00/car) across the river to Spain. It leaves every 30 minutes from 8:00 to 22:00 May-October and 8:00 to at least 20:00 in the off-season. Despite the frequency of ferries, cars can be backed up several hours. The ferry isn't always loaded in an orderly first-come, first-served manner, so if you see a line of cars moving, get in it. Once across the river to Ayamonte, there's a great highway straight into Sevilla (two hours). At Sevilla, follow the signs to "centro ciudad" (city center).

Buses and trains leave almost hourly, connecting most towns along the south coast from Sagres to Vila Real, where you catch the ferry to Ayamonte, Spain. Vila Real has two stops: central and the ferry dock. Take the second stop. From Ayamonte, the Spanish border town, catch a bus or train to Huelva (five buses per day), where you change to Sevilla. Consider hitching a ride from the ferry traffic instead. Remember, you lose an hour when you cross into Spain, so set your watch ahead. (Note: In 1989, there is supposed to be a new bridge, which will make all this very easy.)

Sightseeing Highlights
▲ **Lagos**—The major town and resort on this end of the Algarve is actually a pleasant place. The old town is a whitewashed

jumble of bars, funky crafts shops, outdoor restaurants, and sunburned tourists. The church of San Antonio and the adjoining regional museum are worth a look. Every summer Saturday at 16:00, Lagos has a small for-tourists bullfight in its dinky ring. Seats are a steep 2,200 escudos, but the show is a thrill. If you always felt sorry for the bull, this is Toro's Revenge; in a Portuguese bullfight, the matador is brutalized. Lagos is understandably famous (and crowded) for its beautiful beaches and rugged cliffs.

▲▲ **Tavira**—Straddling a river, with a lively park, market, and boats in its waterfront center, Tavira is a low-rise, easygoing alternative to the other more aggressive Algarve resorts. Tavira has a great beach island (catch the bus to Quatro Aguas from Praça da Republica and then the five-minute ferry ride to Ilha da Tavira).

Those without a car will find Tavira easier to manage than Salema, with a direct Lisbon train connection, easier trip to Sevilla, and a still good—if not so magic—small-townish Algarve atmosphere. The train station is a ten-minute walk from the town center.

Tavira has several good hotels. My favorite is the inexpensive Lagaos Bica (Rua Almirante Candido dos Reis 24, 8800 Tavira, tel. 22252). This residencia is clean, friendly, some English is spoken, and it offers a communal refrigerator, rooftop patio, courtyard garden, laundry privileges, and a good restaurant downstairs. Also a good value in the moderate price range is the new Residencia Princesa do Gilão, which faces the river in the town center (Rua Borda de Agua de Aguilar, tel. 22665). It offers bright, cheery, modern rooms, some with balconies and a view, and an English-speaking management. The tourist office is open daily from 9:00 to 19:00 and can set you up in a cheap room in a private home (tel. 22311).

Sevilla

For the tourist, this big city is small. Think of things relative to the river and the cathedral—which is as central as you can get. The major sights surround the cathedral. The central boulevard, Avenida de la Constitución (tourist information, banks, post office, etc.), zips right by the cathedral to the Plaza Nueva (shopping district). Nearly everything is within easy walking distance. Taxis are cheap, friendly, and thrilling.

Parking: Sevilla is Spain's capital of splintered windshields. The cars of tourists hate it. Many risk it and win. The more prudent pay nearly $10 per day and park in the garages at Plaza Nueva or near the bullring. Paseo de Cristobal Colón ("Christopher Columbus" in Spanish) is particularly dangerous in the summer.

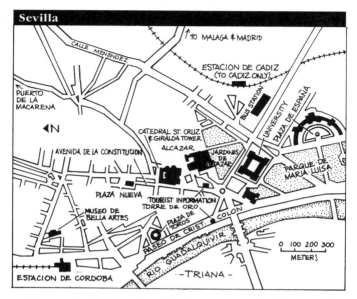

The very helpful tourist office is near the cathedral toward the river and is open daily 9:30-19:00 (tel. 221404). Pick up the Sevilla map/guide with hours of sights and advice for evening fun, "The Route of the White Towns" brochure, and confirm tomorrow's schedule.

Accommodations

Sevilla has plenty of $15-$25 doubles. The best neighborhoods are Santa Cruz (lots of *hostales* and *fondas*, traffic-free, great atmosphere) and within the triangle between the Cordoba Station, the bullring, and the Plaza Nueva. There are many budget hotels along Calle Zaragoza a few blocks off the Plaza Nueva; the farther they are from the plaza, the cheaper they get.

Room rates jump way up during the two Sevilla fiestas (roughly December 20 to January 4 and April 23 to May 7). Otherwise, April, May, September, and October are busiest and most expensive. June, July, and August are cheaper, and empty rooms abound. November through March is the off-season.

The **Hostal Goya** (inexpensive, Mateos Gago 31, tel. 211170) has a great location two minutes down the street from the cathedral, with a cozy courtyard and a friendly, helpful staff. Ground floor rooms are noisy and stuffy.

Hostal Monreal (inexpensive, Rodrigo Caro 8, tel. 214166) also has an excellent locale. It is simple, clean, and friendly.

Head down Mateos Gago from the cathedral and take the first right.

The **Hotel Residencia Murillo** (moderate, Lope de Rueda 7, tel. 216095) is big, dripping with decoration, and in the heart of the Santa Cruz district. It's very hotelly, with "Murillo palette" key chains.

Hotel Residencia Doña María (expensive, Don Remondo 19, tel. 224990) is just off the cathedral square, Plaza Vírgen de los Reyes. This is a wonderful splurge. It brags "very modern but furnished in an ancient style," has four-poster beds, armoirs, a swimming pool, and a view of Giralda Tower.

Hostal Arias (inexpensive, Calle Mariana de Pineda 9, tel. 218389) is clean and quiet, with hard beds and a hard to beat location near the Alcazar toward the river. There are two other inexpensive hotels on this peaceful, but central, street.

Food
For tapas, there are several good barhopping areas.

Barrio Santa Cruz: Your best bet is the **Bodega** right on Mateos Gago, two blocks from the cathedral. Also check out **Lucas' Bar**, a hole in the wall (actually 8 Doncellas) near the Plaza Santa Cruz. Lucas's sketches cover the walls, and he's an artist behind the bar as well.

Triana District (on the other side of the river): Classy bars line the river, while workingman's places are one block in. **La Taberna** (half-block back, between the two bridges, next to the police station) is cheap, youthful, and lively after 23:00.

The area one block west of Avenida de la Constitución: Cross Puente Isabel II (bridge) to the bar in the yellow clock tower, **Sevilla-Sanlucar-Mar**. It's spectacularly decorated, with a roof garden and great views of the river and old town. Many other good bars are nearby, especially **Kiosko Las Flores**.

For a non-tapas meal, there are plenty of places in the Cathedral/Santa Cruz area, which is touristy but reasonable.

For dinner, if you're tired of tapas, you can splurge at the **Río Grande** restaurant across the river (turn right after crossing Puente de San Telmo) with its shady deck over the river—good view, good food, and good service, open 20:00 ($15-$20). Or eat the same thing—with the same view but fewer tablecloths—next door at the self-service **El Puerto** for a third the price. You might try the **Buffet Libre** on Calle Mateos Gago or the **Cervecería Giralda** (at Calle Mateo Gago 1, near the cathedral), a local favorite with great atmosphere and tapas. In the Barrio Santa Cruz, **La Posada** serves fine, inexpensive meals in a wonderful atmosphere—outdoors, with a view of Giralda, and swallows and bats circling above. In Sevilla, dinner starts no earlier than 20:30.

DAY 14
SEVILLA

"Sevilla doesn't have ambience, it *is* ambience."
—James A. Michener

Suggested Schedule

8:00	Breakfast in hotel, or go local in small bars between Paseo de Cristobal Colon and cathedral.
9:00	Alcazar and garden—go early to beat the crowds and heat.
11:00	Cathedral and Giralda Tower. Tour this giant church. Climb the tower. What a view!
13:00	Barrio de Santa Cruz. Stroll through the old Jewish Quarter, peek into private patios, feel the atmosphere.
14:00	Lunch in Santa Cruz or picnic at Plaza de España in the shady Maria Luisa Park. It's siesta time anyway, and nothing's happening until 15:30 or 16:00, especially in summer.
16:00	Shopping. Taxi to the Plaza Nueva, have a *café con leche* and just stroll.
17:00	La Macarena. Take a cab to the Weeping Virgin. Explore behind the altar. (Speedy ones can taxi to the nearby Bellas Artes Museum.)
Evening	Relax at the hotel, stroll through the Barrio de Santa Cruz and up toward the Plaza Nueva for a nightly people parade. By then it's time to dine. Flamenco is best around midnight. Tourist shows start at 21:00, spontaneous combustion in bars at 23:00.

Sevilla

This is the city of flamenco, Carmen, Don Giovanni, and, of course, its barber. While Granada has the great Alhambra, Sevilla has a soul. It's a great-to-be-alive-in kind of place.

Sevilla boomed when Spain did. She was the gateway to the New World. Explorers like Amerigo Vespucci and Magellan sailed from her great river harbor. Sevilla's Golden Age, with its New World riches and great local artists (Velázquez, Murillo, Zurbarán) ended when the harbor silted up and the Spanish Empire crumbled.

Today, Sevilla (pop. 680,000) is Spain's fourth largest city and

Andalusia's number one city. She buzzes with festivals, life, and color. In 1992 (500 years after Columbus rediscovered America) she'll host the World's Fair, and she's already gearing up for this grand six-month-long festival.

Sightseeing Highlights

▲▲ Cathedral—The third largest church in Europe (after St. Peter's and St. Paul's) was built that way on purpose. When the Catholics ripped down a mosque on the site in 1401, they said, "Let us build a cathedral so huge that anyone who sees it will take us for madmen." Though no longer the largest, this late-Gothic wonder remains among the ugliest, in a fascinating way. Don't miss the royal chapel, the sanctuary, the treasury or Columbus's tomb. Open daily 10:30-13:00 and 16:30-18:30, Sundays 10:30-13:00 only, 200 pesetas. The informative private guides charge 1,800 pesetas for one to five people for an hour. The incredible *retablo* (paneled altarpiece) has 4,000 pounds of gold, imported in the "free trade" era of Columbus, with 1,500 figures carved by one man over 40 years. In the *tesoro* (treasury), you'll see a graphic head of John the Baptist, the richest crown in Spain (11,000 precious stones and the world's largest pearl, made into the body of an angel), lots of relics (thorns, chunks of the cross, splinters from the Last Supper table), and some of the lavish Corpus Christi festival parade regalia.

▲ Giralda Tower—Formerly a Moorish minaret that called the Muslims to prayer, it became the cathedral's bell tower after the Reconquista. Notice the beautiful Moorish simplicity as you climb to its top, 100 yards up, for a grand city view. The spiraling ramp is designed to accommodate riders on horseback. Orient yourself from this bird's-eye perspective. Open the same hours (use the same ticket) as the cathedral.

▲▲▲ Alcazar—Much of this lavish Moorish palace was rebuilt by the Christians. The Alcazar is an impressive collection of royal courts, halls, patios, and apartments, in many ways as splendid as Granada's more famous Alhambra. The garden is full of tropical flowers, wild cats, cool fountains, and hot tourists. Try to enjoy it in peace at 9:00. Open 9:00-12:45 and 15:00-17:30, 150 pesetas.

▲▲ Barrio de Santa Cruz (the old Jewish Quarter)—Even if it is a little overrestored, this classy world of lanes too narrow for cars, whitewashed houses with wrought-iron latticework, and azulejo-covered patios is a great refuge from the summer heat and bustle of Sevilla. There are plenty of tourist shops, small hotels, and flamenco bars.

University—Today's university was yesterday's *fabrica de tabacos*, which employed 10,000 young female *cigareras*—

including Bizet's Carmen. It's the second-largest building in Spain, after El Escorial. Wander through its halls as you walk to the Plaza de España. The university's bustling café is a great place for cheap tapas, beer, wine and conversation, and there are plenty of student bars and atmosphere between here and the river.

Bellas Artes Museum—This is Sevilla's top collection of art, with 50 Murillos and some Velázquez paintings. Tuesday-Friday 10:00-14:00, probably 16:00-19:00, Saturdays and Sundays 10:00-14:00, 250 pesetas.

▲ **Virgen de la Macarena**—This altarpiece statue of the Weeping Virgin—complete with crystal teardrops—leads Sevilla's Holy Week processions. She's very beautiful in her special chapel just off the Puerta Macarena. Tour the exhibits behind the altar and go upstairs for a closer look at Mary. Take a taxi. Open 9:00-13:00 and 17:00-21:00. The treasury is open 9:00-12:30 and 17:30-19:30, 100 pesetas.

Bullfights—The most artistic and traditional bullfighting in Spain is done in Sevilla, with fights on most Sundays (and some Thursdays), April-October. (Information: tel. 223152.)

▲ **Plaza de España**—For great people-watching, visit this lovely square made from historic blue and white tiles. Both the square and the nearby María Luisa Park are the remains of a 1929 fair that was killed by the Depression.

Real de la Feria—These fairgrounds, across the river from María Luisa Park, are a very popular student hangout each summer evening.

Evenings and Flamenco—Sevilla is a town meant for strolling. The area around the Plaza Nueva thrives throughout the evening. Spend some time rafting through this sea of humanity.

For a tourist-oriented flamenco show, your hotel can get you nightclub show tickets for about 1,900 pesetas, including a drink. Try La Trocha (Ronda de Capuchinos 23, tel. 355028, 21:00-2:00) or Los Gallos (Plaza de Santa Cruz 11, tel. 216981, 21:30-23:30 and 23:30-2:00). These prepackaged shows can be a bit sterile, but I find Los Gallos professional and riveting.

The best flamenco erupts spontaneously in bars throughout the old town. Just follow your ears in the Barrio de Santa Cruz. Calle Salados, near Plaza de Cuba across the bridge, is also good. Flamenco rarely rolls before midnight.

Shopping—Two fine pedestrian streets (Velázquez/Tetuan and Sierpes) that branch off Plaza Nueva are packed with people and shops. Both streets end up at Sevilla's top department store, El Corte Inglés. While small shops close between 13:00 and 16:00 or 17:00, El Corte Inglés stays open (and air-conditioned) right through the siesta. It has a good, but expensive, restaurant.

SEVILLA, PUEBLOS BLANCOS, AND ARCOS

Today is small Andalusian hill town day. Leave Sevilla early and wind through the golden hills of the "Ruta de Pueblos Blancos" in search of the most exotic whitewashed villages. After several short stops, set up in the capital of the "Pueblos Blancos," Arcos de la Frontera.

Suggested Schedule

8:00	Breakfast and depart.
9:30	Zahara.
11:00	Drive to Grazalema.
12:30	Lunch and wander in Grazalema.
15:00	Drive to Arcos de la Frontera.
16:00	Set up in hotel, climb the bell tower(s), explore the town, have dinner at the convent.

Transportation

The remote hill towns of Andalusia are a joy to tour—only by car and with Michelin map #446. Drivers can zip south from Sevilla on A4. About halfway to Jerez, at Las Cabezas, take C343 to Villamartin. From there, circle scenically (and clockwise) through the thick of the Pueblos Blancos—Zahara, Grazalema, Ubrique, and El Bosque—to Arcos. You'll find good roads and sparse traffic. You'll also find the "Ruta de Pueblos Blancos" pamphlet, which you picked up at the Sevilla tourist office, very handy. Driving in Arcos is like threading needles with your car while giggling—don't even try. Circle around to enter the town from the west end and park as centrally as you comfortably can.

Those without a car should consider whether to rent one (in Jerez), skip all but Arcos, or allow an extra day to manage the miserable public transportation schedules. Hitchhiking is dreadful. There are five buses a day from Sevilla to Jerez and five from Jerez to Arcos. The Sevilla bus station is on Plaza de San Sebastian, a five-minute walk from the Alcazar.

Train connections from Sevilla's Córdoba station are very good: to Madrid, four a day, 8-10 hours; to Córdoba, two a day, 4½ hours; to Málaga, two a day, 3½ hours. There is a *directo* to Granada, 7:20-12:10—consider this if you need to streamline your trip, skipping the beaches and Andalusian towns. As in several Spanish train stations, there may be no baggage lockers available because of bomb threats.

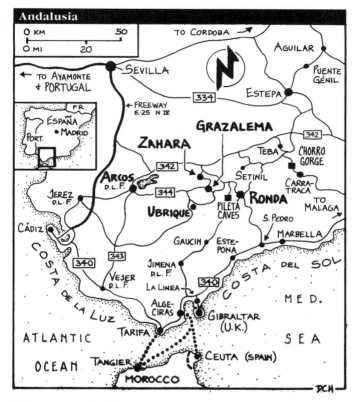

Andalusia

O KM 50
O MI 20

TO CORDOBA

AGUILAR

TO AYAMONTE & PORTUGAL

PUENTE GÉNIL

ESPAÑA • MADRID
FR.
PORT.

SEVILLA

← FREEWAY E·25 N IV

334

ESTEPA

GRAZALEMA

342

ZAHARA

TEBA

CHORRO GORGE

342

ARCOS D.L.F.

SETINIL

CARRA-TRACA

JEREZ D.L.F.

344

RONDA

UBRIQUE

PILETA CAVES

TO MALAGA

CÁDIZ

343

340

GAUCIN

ESTE-PONA

S. PEDRO

MARBELLA

COSTA DEL SOL

VEJER D.L.F.

JIMENA D.L.F.

LA LINEA

340

COSTA

M E D.

DE

LA

LUZ

ALGE-CIRAS

GIBRALTAR (U.K.)

ATLANTIC

TARIFA

S E A

OCEAN

TANGIER

CEUTA (SPAIN)

MOROCCO

DCH

Sightseeing Highlights

▲ **Zahara**—This tiny town with a tingly setting under a Moorish castle (worth the climb) has a spectacular view. Zahara is a fine overnight stop for those who want to hear only the sounds of wind, birds, and elderly footsteps on ancient cobbles. The Hostal Marques de Zahara (moderate, San Juan 3, tel. 956/137261) and the homier Pensión Gonzalo next door (inexpensive, tel. 956/137217) are fine values.

▲ **Grazalema**—Another postcard-pretty hill town, Grazalema offers a royal balcony for a memorable picnic, a square where you can watch local old-timers playing cards, and plenty of quiet, whitewashed streets to explore. The town has several places that rent *camas*, as well as the comfortable Hostal Grazalema (moderate, tel. 111342).

▲▲ **Arcos de la Frontera**—Arcos, smothering its hilltop and tumbling down all sides like an oversized blanket, is larger than

the other towns but equally atmospheric. The old center is a
labyrinthine wonderland, a photographer's feast. Its spectacular
location on a pinnacle overlooking a vast Andalusian plain is
best appreciated from the tops of its two church bell towers.
You can climb each bell tower, passing through the tower
keeper's home. For a tip, he will give you a key and direct you
skyward. Sit alone on the top. Brace your ears at the shattering
top of each hour, and don't play with the big, old clappers. The
church interiors are also worth a look—Zubarán painting,
bones, relics, and Madonnas.

Many towns have "de la Frontera" in their names. They were
often established on the front line of the centuries-long fight to
reconquer Spain from the Muslims, who were slowly pushed
back into Africa.

Just past Arcos on the road to Ronda (C344) is a reservoir
(Embalse de Arcos) in a pine forest with a great beach. A swim
here is refreshing, and if you decide to extend your siesta, you'll
find good beds and meals at Mesón del Brigadier.

Accommodations in Arcos

Arcos is just being discovered, so it's weak on hotel and restaurant choices. There are only the "convent" and a very expensive
parador in the old town. A cluster of room-and-board options
can be found at the west end of town, a five-minute walk from
the center. (Tourist office: tel. 956/702264.)

Hotel Los Olivos (moderate, San Miguel 2, tel. 956/700811)
is a bright, cool, and airy new place with a fine courtyard, roof
garden, bar, view, friendly English-speaking folks, and easy
parking. This is a poor man's parador—it's not cheap, but well
worth it, if only for the big American breakfast with cookies
available if you're good.

Hotel Restaurant "El Convento" (moderate, Maldonado 2,
tel. 956/702333) next to the parador deep in the old town, is the
same quality and nearly as expensive as Los Olivos. There are
only four rooms, two with incredible view balconies. See restaurant listing below.

Fonda del Comercio (cheap, Calle Corredera 15, at the west
end of town, tel. 700057) is big, old, and simple, with no water
in the rooms and saggy beds.

Fonda de las Cuevas (cheap, 50 yards downhill from Fonda
del Comercio) has no phone and is very simple but, with its
nice sundeck, better than Comercio.

Food

The parador is very expensive. The **Restaurante El Convento**
(near the parador) has a wonderful atmosphere. The gracious
lady who runs it is María Moreno Moreno (reminds me of Olive

Oyl, her husband even faintly resembles Popeye). The food is good but not cheap. The 1,000-peseta menu of the day is the best value, including a fine red house wine and special local circular breadsticks (picas de Arcos).

The **Café Bar El Faro** (Debajo del Corral 16) is also good. Taste the great tapas at **Alcaravan** in the west end of town.

Other Andalusian Sightseeing Highlights
There are plenty of undiscovered and interesting hill towns to explore. I found that about half the towns I visited were worth remembering. Unfortunately, good information on the area is very rare. The green Michelin guide skips the region entirely. A good map, the tourist brochure, and a spirit of adventure work fine. Here are some of my favorite finds for those of you who have more time:

Estepa—Except for the busy truck route that skirts the town, peace abounds. Estepa hugs a small hill halfway between Córdoba and Málaga. Its crown is the convent of Santa Clara, worth five stars in any guidebook but found in none. Enjoy the territorial view from the summit, then step into the quiet spiritual perfection of this little-known convent. Just sit in the chapel all alone and feel the beauty soak through your body.

Evening is prime time in Estepa—or any Andalusian town. The promenade, or *paseo*, begins as everyone gravitates to the central square. Estepa's spotless streets are shined nightly by the feet of ice cream-licking strollers. The whole town strolls—it's like "cruising" without cars. Buy an "ice cream bocadillo" and follow suit. The barber of Estepa—a real artist—has a shop right on the square. Make a friend and get a trim. (Driving: Sevilla to Estepa, 2½ hours on N334. Estepa to Ronda, 2 hours on N334, N342 to Campillos, and C341 into Ronda.)

Ortegicar—This teeny six-horse, ten-dog complex of buildings around a castle keep is located a half-mile off C341 on a dirt road, seven miles north of Cuevas del Becerro on the way to Ronda. The nearest train station is La Ronda, seven miles away. Hitch from there.

South of Estepa is the hill-capping village of **Teba** and the interesting towns of **Menzanares** and **Carratraca**. Skip the Chorro Gorge—it's not worth the drive unless you're a real gorge-ophile.

To the north, **Aguilar de la Frontera** and **Puente-Genil** are interesting. Aguilar has a pleasant square, outdoor dancing, and people who are fascinated by tourists with hairy legs.

Jerez, Home of Sherry
A great freeway connects Sevilla and Jerez de la Frontera. Jerez, with nearly 200,000 people, is your typical big-city mix of

industry, garbage, and dusty concrete suburbs, but it has one popular claim to touristic fame—it's the home of sherry. If you're interested, stop at Harveys of Bristol (C. Arcos 53, tel. 346000, two-hour English tours, no reservations required, closed most of August), the Bodega of Pedro Domenca (Calle San Ildefonso 3, outside of town on the road to Cadiz, tel. 331900, open Monday-Saturday 9:30-12:30, closed July, reservations required). Pedro is the world's biggest producer of sherry and brandy. A free guided tour will show you the whole enchilada, including a peek at the oldest sherry in the world, 240 years old. After the one-hour tour, you're rewarded with samples to taste. There are several bodegas with tours and tasting (try Gonzalez Byas at Manuel Maria Gonzalez 12, tel. 340000, and Sandeman at C. Pizarro, tel. 331100). The local tourist office and many travel agencies have maps and listings. Most bodegas close in August.

Ronda
Ronda is the capital of the "white towns." With 40,000 people it's one of the largest, and since it's within easy day-trip range of the "Costa del Turismo," it's very crowded. Still, it has the charm, history, and bus and train connections to make it a good stop.

Ronda's main attractions are the gorge it straddles, the oldest bullring in Spain, and an interesting old town. Ronda's breathtaking ravine divides the town's labyrinthine Roman/Moorish quarter and its new, noisier and more sprawling Mercadillo quarter. A graceful eighteenth-century bridge connects the two halves. Most things of touristic importance are clustered within a few blocks of this bridge—the bullring, view, tourist office, post office, and hotels.

The train and bus stations are 15 minutes by foot from the bridge in the new town. The tourist office is on the square opposite the bridge. (Open Monday-Friday 10:00-14:30 and sometimes 17:00-19:00, tel. 871272.)

Accommodations in Ronda
Pension La Española (cheap, José Aparicio 3, tel. 871052) has a perfect location just off Plaza España opposite the bridge. Its balcony, with a view of the peaceful sunset on mountains, makes it very popular.

Hotel Residencia Polo (moderate, Padre Mariano Soubirón 8, tel. 872447) is two blocks from the bullring. This Old World hotelesque place with its good restaurant is classy and comfortable, not quite stodgy. Rates are cheaper in June and July.

The friendly **Huéspedes Atienza** (cheap, Calvo Asencio 3,

tel. 875236) is in a great paseo part of new town, four minutes from the bridge.

The place with the blue CH plaque on the main square (Plaza de España) is a bit wacky—no phone, no English, very cheap. Check it out.

The best splurge is the royal **Reina Victoria** (expensive, Jerez 24, tel. 871240) hanging over the gorge at the edge of town. It has a great view—Hemingway loved it—but you'll pay for it.

Ronda is most crowded from mid-March through May and August through September. June and July are not bad. Off-season is from November through mid-March.

Food

Try to avoid the tourist traps. One block from the bullring, the Plaza del Socorro has plenty of cheap tapa bars and restaurants. **Las Cañas** at Duque de la Victoria 2 on the corner of the plaza is small, simple, and serves good food. The **Restaurant Alhambra** (Pedro Romero 9) serves a fine 800-peseta, three-course dinner (their mussels and mousse are excellent).

Side Trip: Pileta Caves

The Cuevas de la Pileta are about the best look a tourist can get at prehistoric cave painting these days. The cave, complete with stalagmites, bones, and 25,000-year-old paintings, is 17 miles from Ronda. By car, it's an interesting drive: go north on C339, exit toward Benoajan, then follow the signs, bearing right just before Benoajan, up to the dramatic dead end. Or take the train to Benoajan (tricky scheduling, get help in Ronda's station) and hike two hours uphill to the caves.

The farmer who lives down the hill leads groups through from 9:00 to 14:00 and 16:00 to 19:00. His grandfather discovered the caves. If he's not there, the sign says to yell for him. He is a master at hurdling the language barrier, and as you walk the cool kilometer he'll spend an hour pointing out lots of black and red drawings (five times as old as the Egyptian pyramids) and some weirdly recognizable natural formations like the Michelin man and a Christmas tree. The famous caves at Altamira are closed, so if you want to see Neolithic paintings in Spain, this is a must.

ARCOS DE LA FRONTERA TO TARIFA

Today you get your last dose of Andalusian hill life before taking the short drive to the least touristy piece of Spain's generally over-touristy south coast—the whitewashed port of Tarifa.

Transportation: Arcos to Tarifa (80 miles)
The drive from Arcos south is easy and direct (Arcos-Jerez, and south on E25 past Vejer) or rugged, twisted, and scenic (through the mountains past the photogenic town of Jimena on C3331). The latter route will mean driving the Algeciras-Tarifa road twice.

By bus, there are almost constant connections to Jerez. Seven buses a day go to Cadiz. There are eight buses a day from Cadiz to Tarifa and Algeciras.

Sightseeing Highlights
▲ **More "Route of the White Villages"**—Vejer de la Frontera will lure all but the very jaded off the highway just 20 miles north of Tarifa. Vejer is situated spectacularly with everything you're looking for in a great Andalusian village—a Moorish castle, an interesting church, a tangle of cobbled lanes, sun-baked houses, and friendly pensions or private residences to sleep in.

▲▲ **Tarifa**—This most southerly city in all of Europe is a pleasant alternative to gritty, noisy Algeciras. It's an easygoing, almost Arabic-looking town with a lovely beach, a fine old castle, plenty of boats to Morocco, restaurants sinking in fresh seafood, and inexpensive places to sleep. As I stood on the town promenade under the castle looking out at almost touchable Morocco across the Strait of Gibraltar, I only regretted that I didn't have this book to steer me clear of wretched Algeciras on earlier trips. Tarifa is the jumping-off point for any Moroccan side trip.

Tarifa has no blockbuster sights. Its so-so castle, named after

Guzmán el Bueno (a general who gained fame by proudly refus-
ing to negotiate with his enemies as they killed his son) is surrounded by the cool lanes and whitewashed houses that, if you
get lost enough, seem a lot like Morocco. A few minutes from
downtown is a pleasant sheltered beach, Playa Chica, and just
beyond that beach is a wild and desolate stretch of pristine
shoreline, the Playa de Lances.

Tarifa's main harbor activity seems to be the thrice daily coming and going of the boat to Tangiers. Drop in as soon as possible to buy tomorrow's ticket to Africa.

Accommodations in Tarifa

La Casa Concha Pensión (cheap, San Rosendo 4, tel. 784931)
is a funky little place two blocks from the cathedral.

Fonda Villanueva (inexpensive, G. Queipo de Llano 11, tel.
684149), just next to the old gate of town (Puerta de Jerez), is
friendly, though no English is spoken.

The motel-style **Hostal Tarik** (moderate, Calle San Sebastián
32, tel. 685240), three minutes from the old town gate, has
rooms opening right onto the street.

Hostal La Mirada (inexpensive, Calle San Sebastián 48, tel.
684427), 300 meters toward Cadiz from the old town gate, is
very new and has some sea-view rooms.

The new, cheery, family-run **Hostal Avenida** (moderate,
Calle Pío XII, just off Batalla del Salado, the road to Cadiz, tel.
684818) is very clean and comfy.

Food

The **Chan Bar Restaurant**, on the road to Cadiz just outside
Puerta de Jerez, serves a fine, cheap menu. You'll find good
tapas throughout the old town and good seafood in places
around Plaza San Mateo.

MOROCCO!

Now, for something entirely different, plunge into Africa for a day. The one-day excursions from Tarifa are well organized, reliable, and, given the steep price of the boat passage alone, a good value for those who can spare only a day for Morocco.

Suggested Schedule	
9:30	Board boat.
11:00	Arrive in Tangiers, meet bus and guide, tour city, lunch, see countryside, shop.
16:00	Back on boat, sail Strait of Gibraltar back home.
18:00	Relax in Tarifa.

Morocco in a Day

There are many ways to experience Morocco, and a day in Tangiers is probably the worst, but if all you have is a day, this is a real and worthwhile adventure. Tangiers is the Tijuana of Morocco, and everyone there seems to be jumping up and down for you.

For just a day, I'd recommend the tours organized in Tarifa. For about $50 you get a round-trip hydrofoil crossing, a good guide to meet you at the harbor and hustle you through the hustlers and onto your bus, a bus tour of the area's highlights—ritzy neighborhoods, city tour, trip to the desolate Atlantic Coast for some impressively rugged African scenery, the famous ride-a-camel stop, a walk through the *medina* (market) area of Tangiers with a too-thorough look at a carpet shop, a chance to do battle with the sales-starved local merchants, and a great lunch in a palatial Moroccan setting with belly dance entertainment.

This kind of cultural voyeurism is almost like visiting the devil, but it is nonstop action and more memorable than another day in Spain. The shopping is great—bargain hard!

The day trip is so tightly organized you'll hardly have any time alone in Tangiers. For many people, that's just fine. Some, however, spend a night in Tangiers and return the next day. Ask about this at the tourist office in Tarifa.

Itinerary Option: An Extended Tour of Morocco

While the hour-long cruise to Tangiers from southern Spain takes you farther culturally than the trip all the way from the U.S.A. to Spain, you really should seriously consider going deeper into the interior. Morocco is incredibly rich in cultural thrills per minute and dollar—but you'll pay a price in hassles and headaches. It's a package deal and, for many, a great itinerary option.

To get a fair look at Morocco, you must plunge deep, getting past the hustlers and con artists of the north coast (Tangiers, Tétouan). It takes a minimum of four or five days to make a worthwhile visit—ideally seven or eight. Plan at least two nights in either Fès or Marrakech. A trip over the Atlas mountains gives you an exciting look at Saharan Morocco. If you need a vacation from your vacation, check into one of the idyllic Atlantic beach resorts on the south coast. Above all, get past the northern day-trip-from-Spain, take-a-snapshot-on-a-camel fringe.

Suggested Schedule

By Car:

Day 1	Sail as early as possible from Algeciras to Ceuta, drive to Chechaouene. Set up in Hotel Chaouen on main square facing the old town.
Day 2	Drive to Fès. Find hotel. Take orientation tour.
Day 3	Free to explore the Fès medina. Evening classy dinner and cultural show.
Day 4	Drive to Volubilis near Meknès. Tour ancient Roman ruins, possibly stop in cities of Moulay-Idriss and Meknès. Drive back to Chechaouene. Same hotel, possibly reserved from Day 1.
Day 5	Return to Spain.

By Train and Bus:

Day 1	Sail as early as possible from Algeciras to Tangiers. Catch the 4½ -hour train or bus ride to Rabat (Hotel Splendide).
Day 2	Sightsee in Rabat—Salé, King's Palace, royal tomb.
Day 3	Take the train to Casablanca (nothing to stop for), catch the Marrakech Express from there to the "red city." Get set up near the Medina in Marrakech.
Day 4	Free in Marrakech.
Day 5	Free in Marrakech. Night train back to Rabat.
Day 6	Return to Spain.

Orientation (Mental)

Thrills: Morocco *is* culture shock. It makes Spain and Portugal look meek and mild. You'll encounter oppressive friendliness, the Arabic language, the Islamic faith, and ancient cities; it is a photographer's delight, very cheap, with plenty of hotels, surprisingly easy transportation, and a variety of terrain from Swiss-like mountain resorts to fairy-tale, mud brick oasis towns to luxuriously natural beaches to bustling desert markets.

Spills: Morocco *is* culture shock. Many are overwhelmed by its intensity, poverty, aggressive beggars, brutal heat, and slick con men. Most visitors have some intestinal problems (the big "D"). Most women are harassed on the streets by horny, but generally harmless, men. Things don't work smoothly. In fact, compared to Morocco, Spain resembles Sweden for efficiency. The language barrier is a problem, since French, not English, is Morocco's second language, and most English-speaking Moroccans the tourist meets are hustlers.

Leave aggressive itineraries and split-second timing for Germany. Morocco must be taken on its own terms. In Morocco things go smoothly only "In Sha Allah"—if God so wills.

Transportation

Sailing from Spain to Morocco is cheap and easy (two hours, $10/person, $30-$40/vehicle, no reservations needed, ten boats a day). No visa or shots are necessary; just bring your passport.

If possible, buy a round-trip ticket from Spain. I've had departures from Morocco delayed by ticket-buying hassles there. Change money on arrival only at a bank. (Banks have uniform rates. The black market is dangerous.) Change only what you need and keep the bank receipt to reconvert if necessary. Don't leave the country with Moroccan money. Those driving cars should sail to Ceuta, a Spanish possession (ten crossings a day from Algeciras). Crossing the border is a bit unnerving, since you'll be hustled through several bureaucratic hoops. You'll go through customs, buy Moroccan insurance for your car (cheap and easy), and really feel at the mercy of a bristly bunch of shady-looking people you'd rather not be at the mercy of. Most cars are shepherded through by a guy who will expect a tip. Relax, let him grease those customs wheels. He's worth it. As soon as possible, hit the road and drive to Chechaouene, the best first stop for those driving.

Those relying on public transportation should sail to Tangiers (about $16, 2½ hours). Blast your way through customs, listen to no hustler who tells you there's no way out until tomorrow, and walk from the boat dock over to the train station. From there, just set your sights on Rabat. Make Rabat, a dignified European-type town without the hustlers, your get-acquainted stop in Morocco. From Rabat, trains will take you farther south.

Moroccan trains are quite good. Second class is cheap and comfortable. There are only two lines: Oujda-Fès-Meknès-Rabat-Casablanca (seven times a day) and Tangiers-Rabat-Casablanca-Marrakech (three trains daily).

Sightseeing Highlights—Moroccan Towns

▲▲ **Chechaouene**—Just two hours by bus or car from Tétouan, this is the first pleasant town beyond the Tijuana-type north coast. Mondays and Thursdays are colorful market days. Stay in the classy old Hotel Chaouen on Plaza el-Makhzen. This former Spanish parador faces the old town and offers fine meals and a pleasant refuge from hustlers. Wander deep into the whitewashed old town from here.

▲▲▲ **Marrakech**—Morocco's gateway to the south, this market city is a constant folk festival bustling with djelaba-clad Berber tribespeople—a colorful center where the desert, mountain, and coastal regions merge.

The new city has the train station, and the main boulevard (Mohammed V) is lined with banks, airline offices, a post office, a tourist office, and the city's most comfortable hotels.

The old city features the mazelike *medina* (market) and the huge Djemaa el-Fna, a square seething with people, usually resembling a 43-ring Moroccan circus. Near this square you'll find hordes of hustlers, plenty of eateries, and cheap hotels. (To check for bugs, step into the dark hotel room first, flip on the lights, and count 'em as they flee.)

▲▲▲ **Fès**—The religious and artistic center of Morocco, Fès bustles with craftsmen, pilgrims, shoppers, and shops. Like most large Moroccan cities, it has a distinct new town (*ville nouvelle*) from the French colonial period and a more exotic— and stressful—old Arabic town where you'll find the medina. The Fès marketplace is Morocco's best.

▲▲ **Rabat**—Morocco's capital and most European city, Rabat is the most comfortable and least stressful place to start your North African experience. You'll find a colorful market (in the old neighboring town of Salé), several great bits of Islamic architecture (Mausoleum of Mohammed V), the king's palace, mellow hustlers, and comfortable hotels (try Hotel Splendide, the Peace Corps' favorite, at 2 rue Ghazzah, near where Ave. Mohammed V hits the medina, tel. 23283).

Extend your Moroccan trip three or four days with an excursion south over the Atlas mountains. Buses go from Marrakech to Ouarzazate (short stop), then Tinerhir (great oasis town, comfy hotel, overnight stop). Next day, go to Er Rachidia (formerly Ksar es Souk) and take the overnight bus to Fès.

By car, drive from Fès south, overnighting in the small mountain town of Ifrane, and then continue deep into the desert country past Er Rachidia and on to Rissani (market days, Sunday, Tuesday, and Thursday). From there, you can explore nearby mud brick towns still living in the Middle Ages. Hire a guide to drive you past where the road stops, cross-country to an oasis village (Merzouga) where you can climb a sand dune to watch the sun rise over the vastness of Africa. Only a sea of sand separates you from Timbuktu.

Helpful Hints

Friday is the Muslim day of rest when most of the country closes down.

Marijuana (*kif*) is popular, but illegal, in Morocco, as many Americans in local jails would love to remind you. Some dealers who sell it cheap make their profit after you get arrested. Cars and buses are stopped and checked by police routinely throughout Morocco—especially in the north and in the Chechaouene region, Morocco's kif capital.

Bring good information with you from home or Spain. The *Let's Go: Spain, Portugal and Morocco* book is indispensable. The *Rough Guide to Morocco* is also excellent. If you read French, the green Michelin *Morocco* guidebook is great. Buy the best map you can find locally—names are always changing, and it's helpful to have towns, roads, and place-names written in Arabic.

If you're driving, never rely on the oncoming driver's skill. Drive very defensively. Night driving is dangerous. Your U.S. license is all you need. Pay a guard to watch your car overnight.

While Moroccans are some of Africa's wealthiest people, you are still incredibly rich to them. This imbalance causes predictable problems. Wear your money belt, don't be a sucker to clever local con artists, and haggle when appropriate—prices skyrocket for tourists.

You'll attract hustlers like flies at every famous tourist sight. They'll lie to you, get you lost, blackmail you, and pester the heck out of you. Never leave your car or baggage where you can't get back to it without your "guide." Anything you buy in their company gets them a 20 to 30 percent commission. Normally, locals, shopkeepers, and police will come to your rescue when the hustler's heat becomes unbearable. I usually hire a young kid as a guide, since it's helpful to have a translator, and once you're "taken," the rest seem to leave you alone.

Navigate the labyrinthine medinas by altitude, gates, and famous mosques, towers, or buildings. Write down what gate you came in so you can enjoy being lost—temporarily. *Souk* is Arabic for a particular "department" (such as leather, yarn, or metal work) of the medina.

Health

Morocco is much more hazardous to your health than Spain or Portugal. Eat in clean, rather expensive places. Peel fruit, eat only cooked vegetables, and drink reliably bottled water (Sidi Harazem or Sidi Ali). When you do get diarrhea—and you should plan on it—adjust your diet (small and bland, no milk or grease) and replenish lost fluids or fast for a day. Relax, most diarrhea is not exotic or serious—just an adjustment that will run its course.

Language

The Arabic squiggle-script, its many difficult sounds, and the fact that French is Morocco's second language, make communication tricky for us English-speaking monoglots.

A little French will go a long way, but do learn a few words in Arabic. Have your first local friend teach you "thank you," "excuse me," "yes," "no," "okay," "hello," "good-bye," "how are you," and counting to ten. Listen carefully and write the pronunciations down phonetically. Bring an Arabic phrasebook.

Make a point to learn the local number symbols; they are not like ours (which we call "Arabic"). *La* means no. In markets, I sing "la la la la la" to my opponents. *La shokeron* (think "sugar on") means "No, thank you."

GIBRALTAR AND THE COSTA DEL SOL

After your day in Africa, a day in England may sound jolly good. And that's just where you're going today—to the land of tea and scones, fish and chips, pubs and bobbies—Gibraltar. After this splash of uncharacteristically sunny England, enter the bikini-strangled land of basted bodies on the beach, the Costa del Sol. Bed down in this congested region's closest thing to pleasant, the happy town of Nerja, for a firsthand look at Europe's beachy playground.

Suggested Schedule

8:00	Drive to Gibraltar, breakfast British-style. Morning in town, hike to the Rock's summit, enjoy the viewpoints, fish and chips for lunch?
14:00	Drive the length of the very built-up Costa del Sol. Short stop in "Turistamolinos."
18:00	Arrive and set up in Nerja, evening on the "balcony of Europe."

Transportation: Tarifa to Nerja (150 miles)

The short and scenic drive from peaceful Tarifa to the battle-ground of Algeciras takes 30 minutes. Follow the road around the harbor to La Línea, where you'll park your car as close as you can to the Gibraltar border. The border is actually an air-strip, and when the light is green (no airplanes are coming), you simply cross.

There are regular bus connections from Tarifa, Algeciras, and La Línea (the Spanish town on the Gibraltar border). From La Línea, it's a pleasant 30-minute walk into downtown Gibraltar. You'll find plenty of aggressive cabbies at the border who'd love to give you a tour, and for those with more money than time, this can be a fine value.

From Gibraltar, the trip along the Costa del Sol is smooth and easy by car (just follow the coastal highway east). It's more frustrating by bus or train. The super-developed area between Málaga and Fuengirola is well served by trains (twice an hour, 43 minutes from Málaga to Fuengirola) and buses.

The tiny village of Bobadilla is the unlikely hub of Spain's southern train system. Train travelers, never by choice, always have more than enough time to get to know "Bob." From Bobadilla there are several trains daily to and from Málaga (40 miles, 1 hour, buses connect Málaga and Nerja six times a day),

Costa del Sol

DELIGHTFUL
TOLERABLE
AWFUL

SEVILLA
GRANADA
LANJARÓN
CAVES
P U E B L O S
RONDA
MOTRIL
ARCOS
NERJA
SALOBREÑA
B L A N C O S
MÁLAGA
CÁDIZ
S. PEDRO
TORREMOLINOS
VEJER D.L.F.
ESTEPONA
MARBELLA
FUENGIROLA
COSTA DE LA LUZ
ALGE-CIRAS
LA LINEA
C O S T A   D E L   S O L
TARIFA
GIBRALTAR (U.K.)
MEDITERRANEAN SEA
ATLANTIC
CEUTA (SP.)
TANGIER
OCEAN
MOROCCO
0 KM 50 100 150
0 MI 50 100
DCH

Granada (70 miles, 2 hours), Ronda (40 miles, 80 minutes),
Algeciras (120 miles, 3 hours), and Sevilla (100 miles, 2 ½ hours).
The trip from Bobadilla to Málaga via El Choro is one of Spain's
most scenic mountain train rides.

Sightseeing Highlights
▲▲▲ **The Rock and Town of Gibraltar**—The town of
Gibraltar is a fun mix of Anglican properness, "God Save the
Queen" tattoos, military memories, and tourist shops. The Brit-
ish soldiers you'll see are enjoying this cushy assignment in the
Mediterranean sun as a reward for enduring and surviving an
assignment in another remnant of the British Empire—
Northern Ireland. Your Spanish money and English words both
work wonderfully here.

The real highlight is the spectacular Rock itself. From the
south end of Main Street, you can catch the cable car to the top
with a stop at the Apes' Den on the way. From the "Top of the
Rock" you can explore old ramparts, drool at the 360-degree
view of Morocco, the Strait of Gibraltar, Algeciras and its bay,
and the twinkling Costa del Sol arcing eastward. Below you
stretches the giant water "catchment system" that the British
built to catch rain water in the not-so-distant past when Spain
allowed neither water nor tourists to pass across its disputed
border. The views are especially crisp on brisk off-season days.

As you hike down you may get a close encounter with one of
the famous (and very jaded) "Apes of Gibraltar" and notice the
old casements or underground defenses that Britain built into
the Rock to secure its toehold on the Iberian peninsula.

At the Gibraltar Tourist Offices on Mackintosh Square (tel.
75555) and Cathedral Square (tel. 76400), English is spoken
very well.

▲▲ **Costa del Sol**—It's so bad it's interesting. Northern Europeans are sun worshipers, and this is their Mecca. Anything
resembling a quaint fishing village has been bikini-strangled
and Nivea-creamed. Oblivious to the concrete, pollution, ridic-
ulous prices, and traffic jams, they lie on the beach like small
game hens on skewers—cooking, rolling, and sweating.

Where Europe's most popular beach isn't crowded by high-
rise hotels, it's in a freeway chokehold. While wonderfully
undeveloped beaches between Tarifa and Cadiz and east of
Alvieria are ignored, lemmings make the scene where the
coastal waters are so polluted that hotels are required to provide
swimming pools. It's a wonderful study in human nature. For
your Costa del Sol experience, drive from San Pedro de Alcantara to Motril, spending the afternoon and evening at one of the
resorts listed here.

San Pedro de Alcantara—This relatively undeveloped sandy
beach is popular with young travelers heading for Morocco (a
good place to find a partner for a North African adventure). San
Pedro's neighbor is Puerto Banus, "where the world casts
anchor." This luxurious jet-set port complete with casino is a
strange mix of Rolls-Royces, yuppies, boutiques, rich Arabs, and
budget browsers.

Fuengirola/Torremolinos—This is the most built-up part of
the region, where those people most determined to be envied
settle down. It's a bizarre world of Scandinavian package tours,
flashing lights, pink flamenco, multilingual menus, and all-night
happiness. My choice for the Costa del Sol evening is Fuengirola, a Spanish Mazatlán with some less pretentious older
budget hotels a block off the beach. The water here is clean
enough and the nightlife fun and easy.

Nerja—Somehow Nerja, while joining in the high-rise parade,
has actually kept much of its quiet Old World charm. It has a
good beach, a fun evening paseo, culminating in its proud "Balcony of Europe" terrace, and enough nightlife. Nerja's beach
crowds thin as you walk farther from town. The room situation
is tight in the summer, so arrive early, let the tourist office help
you, or follow a local woman to a casa particular or camas.

Almuñecar—Smaller and the least touristy is Almuñecar,
where a tangle of alleys in the old town and a salty fishing village atmosphere survive amid high-rise hotels.

Itinerary Option
To save a day, you could skip the beach and go from Tarifa
directly to Granada by train, bus, or car via Málaga.

Nerja Accommodations

The entire Costa del Tourismo is crowded during peak season. August is most difficult, with July and September also tight. June is less intense and March, April, May, and October are shoulder season when things are manageable. November to February is off-season, when things are quiet and prices are lowest. Remember, prices fluctuate with demand. A $20 double off-season will fetch $30 in the summer.

Nerja has plenty of comfy low-rise, easygoing resort-type hotels. **Hostal Atembeni** (Diputacion 12, tel. 521341), **Hostal Residencia Don Peque** (Diputacion 13, tel. 521318), and **Hostal Residencia Mena** (El Barrio 15, tel. 520541) are all central, pleasant but basic, and inexpensive to moderate in price.

Habitaciones de José Luis Jaime Escobar Compresores y Voladuras (Mendez Nunez 12, tel. 522930) is cheap, clean, and friendly, has more local style, and is an easy eight-minute walk from the town center.

For private accommodations (*casas particulares*), ask around. These private rooms are your cheapest bet. The Nerja tourist office (4 Puerta del Mar, tel. 521531) is open only in summer (10:00-14:00 and 18:00-20:30).

Food

You'll find plenty of lively eateries around the central Balcony of Europe. The **Cou-Cou Rotisserie** is a good place if you feel like chicken. Half a bird costs 400 pesetas.

COSTA DEL SOL TO GRANADA

After a beach-easy morning in Nerja, drop into the immense
Nerja caves and say adios to the Mediterranean as you head
inland through the rugged Sierra Nevada mountains to the
historic city of Granada. The last stronghold of the Moorish
kingdom, Granada still has an exotically tangled Arab quarter,
a great place for dinner, and an Alhambra view.

Suggested Schedule

Morning	Free in town and on beach, or leave early to tour the caves.
13:00	Lunch in Nerja or at the caves.
15:00	Drive to Granada.
17:00	Set up in Granada. Sunset from San Nicolas in Albaicín.
20:00	Dinner in Albaicín.

Transportation: Nerja to Granada (80 miles)
Drive along the coast to Salobrena, catching E103 north for
about 40 miles to Granada. While scenic side trips may beckon,
it's important to arrive in Granada by mid-afternoon to find a
room.

Those without cars will catch one of eight daily buses from
anywhere along the coast, including Nerja, to Granada. From
Nerja it's a two-hour ride.

Sightseeing Highlight
▲▲ **The Caves of Nerja**—These caves have the most impressive pile of stalactites and stalagmites I've seen anywhere in
Europe, with huge cathedrals and domed stadiums of caverns
filled with expertly backlit formations and very cavey music—
well worth the time and money. (Daily 9:30-21:00, shorter
hours in off-season.)

Granada
"There's nothing crueler than being blind in Granada," they say.
It is a fascinating city, with a beautiful Sierra Nevada backdrop,
the Alhambra fortress glowing red in the evening, and Spain's
best-preserved Moorish quarter.

Orient yourself in Granada with the "T" formed by the two
main drags in town, the Gran Vía de Colón and the Reyes
Católicos. Nearly everything of interest is near these two streets.

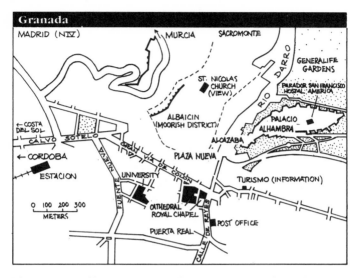

The Reyes Católicos runs up to the Plaza Nueva, where the Darro River takes over. This river gorge splits the two hillsides—the Alhambra on the right and the old Moorish Albaicín quarter on the left. Neither the bus nor the train station is central, but bus #11, from near the cathedral, goes to and from both. By the way, "Granada" means pomegranate and you'll see the city's symbol everywhere.

Accommodations
In Granada, I try to sleep near the Plaza Nueva on Cuesta de Gomerez, the road leading up to the Alhambra. In July and August, rooms and sunstroke victims are plentiful. September, October, and November are more crowded, and you'll want to arrive early or call ahead. Upon arrival, drive, bus, or taxi to the Plaza Nueva. You'll find many small, reasonable hotels to choose from within a few blocks up Cuesta de Gomerez. Here are my choices:

   Hostal Landazur (inexpensive, Cuesta de Gomerez 24, tel. 221406), run by friendly, English-speaking Matilda Landazur, is plain, clean, with a pleasant roof garden. **Hostal Navarro Ramos** (cheap, nearby at 21, tel. 221876) is very simple with no private showers.

   Right on the colorful Plaza Nueva at #4 is **Hotel Residencia Macia** (moderate, tel. 227536). This classy, hotelesque place is clean and modern, with English spoken, and comes with a Yankee breakfast buffet and your choice of a view on the square or a quiet room.

Near the Alhambra, the stately old **Hotel Washington Irving** (expensive, Paseo del Generalife 2, tel. 227550) is pleasant and spacious, offering the best reasonable beds in this prestigious neighborhood. There are two famous, overpriced and difficult-to-get-a-room-in hotels actually within the Alhambra grounds. The **Parador Nacional San Francisco** ($100 doubles, tel. 958/221493) is a converted fifteenth-century convent, usually called Spain's premier parador. You must book ahead to spend the night in this lavishly located, stodgy, classy, and historic place. Do drop in for coffee or a drink and wander around. Also in the Alhambra, just next to the parador, is **Hostal America** ($80 doubles, tel. 958/227471), which is small (just 14 rooms), elegant, snooty, and very popular. Advance bookings are necessary, and you are virtually required to have dinner there.

Delightfully located back in the real world on a lively, but traffic-free, square behind the cathedral, a ten-minute walk from Plaza Nueva, is **Hostal Residencia Los Tilos** (inexpensive, Plaza Bib-Rambla 4, tel. 266712). This is a great shopping and people-watching area.

Food
The best cheap places are in the Albaicín quarter, where there is both great food and wonderful atmosphere. From the San Nicolas viewpoint, head a few blocks north (away from the Alhambra) to Calle Pages. Try the quiet patio in the otherwise unquiet **Café-Bar Higuera**, just off Plaza Fatima.

For a memorable orgy of seafood specialties at a reasonable price with great outdoor tables in a colorful square atmosphere, eat at **El Ladrillo** (Placeta de Fatima just off Calle Pages in the Albaicín). Their *media barca* (half boat) is a fishy feast for two.

For a splurge ($15) with a view, try one of the restaurants along the south face of the Alhambra hill near the big, ugly, and red Arab Palace Hotel.

For tapas, prowl through the bars around the Plaza del Campo del Príncipe. For good food on Cuesta de Gomerez, try **Restaurante el Farol** at 10. For a pleasant, shady meal near the Generalife after your Alhambra tour, eat at **La Mimbre La Alhambra**.

There are plenty of good places around the Plaza Nueva. Try **Mesón Andaluz** at Elvira 10 (new, clean, air-conditioned, with few tourists) or **Restaurant Bar León** just west of Plaza Nueva at Calle Pan 3 for good tapas, cheap meals, and a friendly atmosphere.

GRANADA

We'll have all day to explore this city's incomparable Alhambra Palace and its exotically tangled Arabic Quarter, flirt with the Gypsies, and stroll with the Granadines.

Suggested Schedule

8:00	Breakfast.
9:00	Wander, stroll, and shop in pedestrian zone.
11:00	Tour royal chapel and cathedral.
12:30	Picnic in Generalife, enjoy garden.
14:00	Tour Alhambra.

Sightseeing Highlights
▲▲▲ **Alhambra and Generalife**—The last and greatest Moorish palace is one of Europe's top sights, attracting up to 20,000 visitors a day. Nowhere else does the splendor of Moorish civilization shine so brightly.

The Alhambra, with all due respect, is really a symbol of retreat. Granada was a regional capital for centuries before the Christian Reconquista gradually took Córdoba (1236) and Sevilla (1248), leaving Granada to reign until 1492 as the last Moorish stronghold in Europe. As you tour this grand palace, remember that while Europe slumbered through the Dark Ages, Moorish magnificence blossomed—finely chiseled stucco, plaster stalactites, colors galore, scalloped windows framing Granada views, exuberant gardens, and water are everywhere. Water, so rare and precious in most of the Islamic world, was the purest symbol of life to the Moors. The Alhambra is decorated with water—standing still, running slow and fast, cascading, and drip-dropping playfully.

Buy a guidebook, use the map on the back of your ticket, and climb to the Torre de la Vela (watchtower) for a grand view and orientation.

Don't miss the summer palace, the Generalife (pronounced: hay-nay-rahl-EE-fay). This most perfect Arabian garden in Andalusia was the summer home of the Moorish kings, the closest thing on earth to the Koran's description of heaven. Consider a picnic in the Generalife. Unfortunately, the Generalife fountains run only in the morning.

Guided tours are expensive, and beauty is more important here than history. Use a local guidebook or listen to other groups. Crowds can swamp the Alhambra. To beat the crowds, be at the starting gate at 9:30, skip the Alcazaba, and start out in the Casa Real (Alcazar). You'll do the Alcazaba last and enjoy the rest in precious solitude. All parts of the Alhambra are open daily 9:00-20:00, until 18:00 on Sundays and off-season, 425 pesetas. Your ticket is good for two days. Ask at the tourist office about evening tours and concerts held on most Friday and Saturday evenings. (Note: My suggested schedule ignores this advice, to let you catch work-a-day Granada at its vibrant best and visit the Alhambra when almost nothing else is open.)

▲▲ **Albaicín**—This is one of the best old Moorish quarters in Spain, with thousands of colorful corners, flowery patios, and shady lanes to soothe the twentieth-century-mangled visitor. Climb to the San Nicolas church for the best view of the Alhambra—especially at sunset. Go on a photo safari. Ignore the Gypsies. Women shouldn't wander alone.

For the quickest, most scenic walk up the hill, leave from the west end of the Plaza Nueva on Calle Elvira, then turn right on tiny Calderería Nueva. Follow the stepped street as it slants, winds, and zigzags up the hill. Near the crest, turn right on Camino Nuevo de San Nicolas, walking several blocks to the church's viewpoint. From there, walk north (away from the Alhambra), through the old Moorish wall into the tiny city square. Stop for something to eat or drink here or in one of the many cafés on Calle Pages, two more blocks north. From Calle Pages, you can reach Sacromonte.

▲▲ **Royal Chapel (Capilla Real)** and **Cathedral**—Without a doubt Granada's top Christian sight, this lavish chapel holds the dreams—and bodies—of Queen Isabella and King Ferdinand. Besides the royal tombs, you'll find some great Flemish art, a Botticelli painting, the royal jewels, Ferdinand's sword, and the most lavish interior money could buy 500 years ago. Because of its speedy completion, the chapel is an unusually harmonious piece of architecture. (Open daily 10:30-13:00, 16:00-19:00, 100 pesetas.)

The cathedral, the only Renaissance church in Spain, is a welcome break from the twisted Gothic and tortured Baroque of so many Spanish churches. Spacious, symmetrical, and lit by a stained-glass-filled rotunda, it's well worth a visit. The Renaissance facade and the paintings of the Virgin in the rotunda are by Granada's own Alonso Cano (1601-1661). Open daily 10:30-13:00, 16:00-19:00, 100 pesetas. The coin-op lighting is worthwhile.

☹ **Sacromonte**—Europe's most disgusting tourist trap, famous for its cave-dwelling, foot-stomping, flamenco-dancing Gypsies, is a snakepit of con artists. You'll be teased, taken, and turned away. Venture in only for the curiosity and leave your money in the hotel. Enjoy flamenco in Madrid or Sevilla. Gypsies have gained a reputation (all over Europe) for targeting tourists. Be careful. Even mothers with big eyes and cute babies manage to sneak a hand in your pocket.

Lotería de Ciegos—In Granada you may notice blind men selling lottery tickets with nerve-wracking shouts. This is a form of welfare. The locals never expect to win, it's just sort of a social responsibility to help these people out. The saying goes, *"Dale limosna, mujer, porque no hay nada que ser ciego en Granada"* (Give him a coin, woman, because there's nothing worse than being blind in Granada).

Carthusian Monastery (La Cartuja)—This small church is nicknamed the "Christian Alhambra" for its elaborate white Baroque stucco work. Notice the gruesome paintings of martyrs placidly meeting their grisly fates (in the rooms just off the cloister). It's located a mile out of town—go north on Gran Vía and follow the signs or take bus #8. (Open 11:00-13:00 and 16:00-19:00.)

International Festival of Music and Dance—From mid-June to mid-July you can enjoy some of the world's best classical music in classic settings in the Alhambra at reasonable prices.

GRANADA TO TOLEDO

Today's goal is to travel 250 miles north, lunching in La Mancha country and arriving early enough to get comfortably set up and oriented in the historic, artistic, and spiritual capital of Spain—Toledo.

Suggested Schedule	
8:00	Breakfast and drive north.
12:00	Picnic lunch at Consuegra, tour castles and windmills.
14:00	Drive on to Toledo.
16:00	Arrive in Toledo, confirm plans at tourist office, set up, and enjoy roast suckling pig in a restaurant in the dark medieval quarter.

Transportation: Granada to Toledo (250 miles)

The drive north from Granada is long, hot, and boring. Start early to minimize the heat, and make the best time you can in the direction of Madrid: Granada—Jaén-Bailén—Valdepeñas—Manzanares—Consuegra—Toledo. Past Puerto Lápice, turn off to Consuegra for a lunch stop. Then you're within an hour of Toledo.

Don't go by bus. If limited to public transportation, take the overnight Granada-Madrid train (23:15-8:00). From Madrid there are 15 trains a day to Toledo, one hour and 40 miles to the south. You can take the night train more directly to Toledo, changing in Aranjuez. Make your arrangements at the Granada RENFE office on Calle Reyes Católicos, one block down from Plaza Nueva, open 9:00-15:00 and 17:00-19:00.

La Mancha

Nowhere else is Spain so spacious, flat, and radically monotonous. Except for the red and yellow carpets of flowers that come with the winter rain, La Mancha is a dusty brown.

This is the setting of Cervantes' *Don Quixote*, published in the seventeenth century after England sank the Armada and the Spanish empire began its decline. Cervantes' star character fought doggedly for good and justice and against the fall of Spain. Ignoring reality, Don Quixote was a hero fighting a hopeless battle, a role by no means limited to people in Spain—or to the past. Stark La Mancha is the perfect stage for this sad and futile fight against reality.

The epitome of Don Quixote country, the town of Consuegra must be the La Mancha Cervantes had in mind. Drive up to the ruined twelfth-century castle and string of windmills. It's hot and buggy here, but the powerful view overlooking the village, with its sun-bleached, light red roofs, modern concrete reality, and harsh windy silence, makes for a profound picnic before driving on to Toledo (one hour). The castle belonged to the knights of St. John (twelfth and thirteenth centuries) and is associated with their trip to Jerusalem during the Crusades. Originally built from ruins of a nearby Roman circus, it has been newly restored. The windmills are only 200 to 300 years old (post-Cervantes). In the town center, El Rabano serves good tapas and raciones and reasonably priced menus de la casa.

A desert swim? The fourteen deep blue lagoons of Ruidera are 30 miles east of Manzanares at the beautiful headwaters of the Río Guadino.

Toledo

Lassoed into a tight tangle of streets by the sharp bend of the Tagus River, Toledo has a street plan more medievally confusing than any other Spanish city. But it's a small town, with only 50,000 people, and a joy to cover on foot. Because of the town's popularity with tourists, major sights are well signposted, and most locals can point you in the right direction if you ask.

If you arrive by car, view the city from many angles along the Circunvalación road across the Tagus Gorge. Drive to the Conde de Orgaz Parador just south of town for a great view of Toledo from the balcony (the same view as El Greco's famous *Portrait of Toledo*).

Enter the city by the north gate and park in the open-air guarded lot (cheap, but not safe overnight) or in one of three garages ($6 for 24 hours). The garage and lot just past the Alcazar are easy and as central as you need. The tourist office, just outside the north wall gate, has maps and accommodations lists. (Open Monday-Friday 9:00-14:00 and 16:00-18:00, Saturdays 9:00-13:30, tel. 925/220843.) The handy local guide, "This Is Toledo," sold all over town, explains all the sights (which generally provide no explanation) and gives you a photo to point at and say *"Dónde está?"* when you need directions.

The train station is a long hike from town but easily connected by buses #1, #3, and #5. The bus station, just below Plaza de Zocodover, is much more central. Buses and trains make the 90-minute trip to and from Madrid almost every hour. Buses are more direct.

Orient yourself with a walk past Toledo's main sights. Starting in the Plaza de Zocodover, walk southwest along the Calle de Comercio. After passing the cathedral on your left, follow the

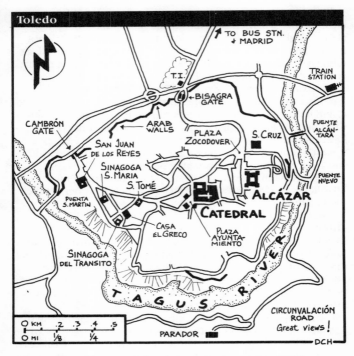

signs to Santo Tome and the cluster of other sights. While
Toledo seems confusing at first glance, this walk shows you that
the visitors' city is basically along one small, but central, street.

Accommodations
By all means spend a night in Toledo. Madrid day-trippers clog
the sunlit cobbles, but Toledo's medieval moon rises after dark.
Because Toledo sees many more day-trippers than overnighters,
accommodations can be tough to find. Budget pensiones are
plentiful but scattered. It's easier to follow a hotel runner to his
place from the Plaza de Zocodover. The tourist office has a list
of private rooms in town.

   Hotel Maravilla (moderately priced, Barrio Rey 7, just
behind the Plaza de Zocodover, tel. 223300) is very Spanish,
central, quiet, convenient, and a fine value. **Fonda Segovia,** at
Calle de Recoletos 2, on a square (from Zocodover, go down
Calle de la Silleria and take the second right, tel. 211124), is
cheap, quiet, clean, and friendly. It's also old, rickety, and dingy,
with saggy beds and memorable balconies.

Pensión Sevillana (Chapineria 4, on north side of cathedral, no phone) is cheap, old, basic, central and has no water in the rooms. Right across from the Alcazar is **Hotel Alfonso VI** (moderate, General Moscardo 2, tel. 222600), a big, touristy, English-speaking place with large, airy rooms, tour groups, and souvenirs for sale all over the lobby.

The best splurge in town is the **Hostal de Cardenal** (expensive, Paseo de Recardo 24, near Puerta Bisagra at the edge of town, tel. 224900). This seventeenth-century palace built into the Toledo wall is quiet and elegant, with a cool garden and a fine restaurant.

The youth hostel, **Residencia Juvenil San Servando**, in the San Servando castle near the train station, over the Puente Viejo (bridge) outside of town (tel. 224554) is lavish but cheap, with small rooms, swimming pool, views, and a good management. They can direct you to nearby budget beds when the hostel is full.

Food

Eating cheaply in Toledo is tough, but the romance of this town always puts me in the mood for a good splurge. Suckling pigs— roasted—are the usual victims of my Toledo splurges. Try **Casa Aurelio** (Plaza Ayuntamiento 8, near the cathedral, call 227716 for a reservation) for great food, moderate prices, and classy atmosphere. Another fine splurge is a meal in the palatial **Hostal de Cardenal Restaurant** (see Accommodations). This hotel's restaurant serves wonderfully prepared local specialties.

You'll find several good budget restaurants behind the Zocodover, including **Maravilla** (Barrio Rey 5, take the alley from Zocodover past Café Casa Telesfor to a small square) and its neighbors. **Restaurant Río** (Calle Nueva 9 behind the Caja Postal) is a good bet for atmospheric and very local-style meals.

For breakfast, **Cafetería Repostería** at Comercio 38 serves fresh croissants and churros. These are about the best churros you'll find—and they still rival lutefisk as the leading European national dish of penitence.

For tapas on a quiet square, stand and admire the cathedral's main portal from Plaza Ayuntamiento, then do an about-face and walk fifty yards down an alley to **El Torreón**. Toledo's yuppies tapa elbows here at night. For Toledo's famous almond-fruity sweet marzipan, try **Casa Telesforo** at Plaza de Zocodover 17, open until 22:00. The bars and cafés on Plaza de Zocodover are reasonable. Sit outside and enjoy the scene.

Picnics are best assembled at the **Mercado Municipal** on Plaza Mayor (on the Alcazar side of the cathedral). This is a fun market to prowl, even if you don't need food.

DAY 22
TOLEDO, RETURN TO MADRID

Tour Toledo, a city of such beauty and historic importance that
the entire town was declared a national monument. Finally,
you'll complete your 22-day circle through Spain and Portugal
by returning to Madrid.

Suggested Schedule

8:30	Breakfast, check out of hotel.
9:30	Santo Tome and El Greco's House.
11:00	Tour cathedral.
13:30	Lunch, siesta, and go shopping.
16:00	Santa Cruz Museum.
18:00	Return to Madrid, where you have a hotel reserved and paid for from the beginning of your trip. (Or spend another evening and night in Toledo, Spain's most magically medieval big town.)

Toledo
Spain's historic capital is 2,000 years of tangled history—
Roman, Visigothic, Moorish, and Christian—crowded onto a
high rocky perch surrounded on three sides by the Tagus River.
It's so well preserved that the Spanish government has forbidden any modern exteriors. Its rich mix of Jewish, Moorish, and
Christian heritage makes it one of Europe's art capitals.
      Toledo was a Visigothic capital way back in 554 and Spain's
political capital until 1561, when it reached its limits of growth,
as defined by the Tagus Gorge, and the king moved to the more
spacious Madrid. Today, in spite of tremendous tourist crowds,
Toledo just takes care of its history and remains much as it was
when El Greco called it home, and painted it, 400 years ago. By
the way, if you like El Greco, you'll love Toledo.

El Greco
Born on Crete and trained in Venice, Domenico Theotocopuli
(people just called him "The Greek") settled in Toledo and
mixed all three regional influences into his palette. From his
Greek homeland he absorbed the solemn, abstract style of
icons. In Venice, he learned the bold use of color and dramatic
style of the later Renaissance. These styles were then fused in
the fires of fanatic Spanish Catholic devotion.
      Not bound by the realism so important to his contemporaries,

El Greco painted dramatic visions of striking colors and figures, with bodies unnatural and elongated as though stretched between heaven and earth. He painted souls, not faces. His work is almost as fresh to us as the art of today, thoroughly "modern" in its disregard of realism.

Sightseeing Highlights
▲▲▲ **Cathedral**—Holy Toledo! Spain's leading Catholic city has a magnificent cathedral. A confusing collage of great Spanish art, it deserves (and, I think, requires) a guided tour. Hire a private guide (or freeload). If the $20 is beyond your budget, gather a small group to split the price—tell them you need it. The cathedral took over 200 years to build, which explains the mix of styles you'll see. Under its 300-foot spire you'll find enough Gothic, Renaissance, and Baroque art to fill a textbook. Your guide will show you elaborate wrought ironwork, lavish wood carving, window after colorful window of 500-year-old stained glass, and a sacristy with a collection of paintings that ranks it among Europe's top museums. All the time I felt my guide's national pride saying, "Look at this great stuff! Why do you tourists get so excited about Michelangelo and Leonardo? Take a look at Spain!" It is interesting how little attention we give the art of Spain's Golden Age. (Open daily 10:30-13:00 and 15:30-19:00, 250 pesetas.)

The cathedral's sacristy has over twenty El Grecos, masterpieces by Goya, Titian, Rubens, Velázquez, Bellini, and a carved St. Francis that could change your life. (Open 10:00-13:00 and 15:30-19:00.) Fernando Garrido, a guide and interpreter who runs a jewelry shop in the cathedral cloister just at the entrance, gives an excellent one-hour tour for 3,000 pesetas. He is an entertaining and friendly character (reminds me of Rodney Dangerfield) and has a wealth of information (tel. 224007). Say "buenos días" to him in his shop and consider enlisting his help.

▲▲ **Santa Cruz Museum**—This great Renaissance hospital building holds twenty-two El Grecos and much more in a tasteful, stately, old classical, music-filled setting. Open Monday-Saturday 10:00-18:30, Sundays 10:00-14:00, 200 pesetas. Use the free English pamphlet. No photos are allowed, but cheap slides are available.

Alcazar—This huge former imperial residence dominates the Toledo skyline. It's entirely rebuilt, but its Civil War exhibits give the visitor a good look at the horrors of Spain's recent past. Open 10:00-14:00 and 16:00-19:00, closed Mondays, 125 pesetas.

▲▲ **Santo Tome**—A simple chapel with probably El Greco's most exciting painting. The powerful *Burial of Count of Orgaz* merges heaven and earth in a way only "The Greek" could. It's so good to see a painting left where the artist put it 400 years ago. Sit here for a while—let the painting perform. Each face is a detailed portrait. Notice the artist's self-portrait looking straight at you (sixth figure in line from the left). The boy in the foreground is El Greco's son. Open Tuesday-Saturday 10:00-13:45 and 15:30-19:00, Sundays 10:00-13:45, closed Mondays, 95 pesetas.

El Greco's House—Although not really his house, it still gives you an interesting look at the interior of a traditionally furnished Renaissance home. You'll see El Greco's masterful *View of Toledo* and portraits of the apostles. Open 10:00-14:00 and 16:00-18:00, closed Sunday afternoons and Mondays, 200 pesetas.

Sinagoga del Transito—This beautiful part of Toledo's Jewish past, built in 1366, is located next to El Greco's house on Calle de los Reyes Católicos. It's open the same hours as El Greco's house.

Shopping—Toledo probably sells as many souvenirs as any city in Spain. This is the best place to buy old-looking swords, armor, maces, medieval-looking three-legged stools and other nouveau antiques. It's also Spain's damascene center, where, for centuries, craftsmen have inlaid black steelware with gold, silver, and copper wire. At Calle Ciudad 19, near the cathedral and Plaza Ayuntamiento, you can see swords and knives being made in the workshop of Mariana Zamorano.

Transportation: Toledo to Madrid (40 miles)
Drive north to Madrid on either N401 or N-IV. The highways converge into M30, which circles Madrid. Follow it to the left ("Nor y Oeste") and take the "Plaza de España" exit to get back to the Gran Vía. Don't hesitate to get as downtown as you can and hire a taxi to lead you back to your car rental turn-in point.

Trains leave regularly for the quick 40-mile Toledo-Madrid trip.

* * *

That's my idea of the most exciting 22 days Spain and Portugal have to offer. I hope you have a great trip—and many more.

BARCELONA

My biggest frustration in putting this 22-day plan together was excluding Barcelona. If you're flying into Madrid, it's nearly 400 miles out of your way. By car it's not worth it, but by train it's just an easy overnight ride away. Coming to Spain from points north, Barcelona is a great and easy first stop.

This capital of the proud and distinct region of Catalonia bubbles with life in its old Gothic Quarter, along its grand boulevards, and around its booming harbor. While Barcelona has an exciting past as a Roman colony, Visigothic capital, and, in modern times, a top Mediterranean trading and manufacturing center, it's most enjoyable to throw out the history books and just drift through the city. If you're in the mood to surrender to a city's charms, let it be in Barcelona.

The soul of Barcelona is in its compact core—the Barrio Gótico (Gothic Quarter) and the Ramblas (main boulevard). This is your strolling, shopping, and people-watching nucleus.

The city's sights are widely scattered, but with a good map and a willingness to figure out the subway and bus system, it's all manageable. Use one of the several helpful tourist offices (there's one in the Sants-Central train station, tel. 4102594) for free maps and accommodations listings.

Barcelona has several train stations. Estación de Francia serves France, Sants-Central serves the south, and the Estación del Norte handles Madrid trains and is also the main bus terminal.

Be on guard. Barcelona's thieves thrive on unwary tourists. More bags and wallets seem to be stolen here than anywhere.

Sightseeing Highlights
▲▲ **The Ramblas**—More than a "Champs Elysées," this grand Barcelonian axis goes from rich at the top to rough at the port. You'll find the grand Opera House, richly decorated churches, plenty of prostitutes, pickpockets, con men and artists, elegant cafés, and great shopping. When Hans Christian Andersen saw this street over a hundred years ago, he wrote that there could be no doubt that Barcelona was a great city. Don't miss "Mumbru," a fascinating old Colonial import shop at Rambla de Estudio 115.

▲▲ **Barrio Gótico**—Bustling with shops, bars, and nightlife, the Gothic Quarter is packed with fourteenth- and fifteenth-century buildings. Highlights are the great cathedral, the Ayuntamiento (old town hall), several palaces and museums, and the Chocolatería Dulcinea on Carrer de Petrixotl, which has been

serving delicious chocolate for 160 years—Spanish style (with water), French (with milk), and Swiss (with cream).
Plaza Real—This square is worth visiting simply for its beauty.
▲ **Gaudi's buildings**—All over town you can find the work of the great Art Nouveau architect, Antoni Gaudi. The most important of his buildings is Sagrada Familia (Sacred Family) Church, open daily 8:00-21:00, winter only until 19:00.
▲ **The Picasso Museum**—This great collection of Picasso's work is a perfect chance to see his earliest paintings and better understand his genius (open Tuesday-Saturday 9:30-13:30 and 16:00-20:30, Sundays 9:30-13:30, Mondays 16:00-20:30).

Accommodations
Barcelona has lots of inexpensive rooms. Your big decision is which neighborhood. The Ramblas and Barrio Gótico areas are in the thick of things with plenty of cheap restaurants and bars and more than their share of theft and grime. Calle Boquería and Calle Escudelleros are two particularly good streets for accommodations.

At Rambla de Canaletas 133 you'll find two basic, cheap, friendly places: **Hostal Noya** (tel. 3014831), and **Hostal Canaletas** (tel. 3015660). The **Colón Hotel** (expensive, Avenida Catedral 7, tel. 3011404) has an elegant Old World style. The **Orient** (moderate, Ramblas 45, tel. 3022558); the **Hostal Rey Don Jaime I** (cheap, Carrer Jaime I 11, tel. 3154161); and **Casa del Metge** (inexpensive, Calle Tapinería 10, tel. 3101590) are also good values.

The Eixample area is a handy, comfortable, and safe hotel area. Try **Hostal-Residencia Palacios** (inexpensive, facing the central tourist office at Gran Vía 629, tel. 3013792).

Barcelona has several youth hostels. **Hostal Verge de Montserrat** (ride bus #28 nearly half an hour to Passeig Nostra Senyora de Coll 41, tel. 2138633) is big, classy, clean, cheap, and usually has beds available.

Food
Barcelona, the capital of Catalonian cuisine, offers a tremendous variety of colorful places to eat. The harbor area is famous for fish. The best tapa bars are in the Barrio Gótico and around the Picasso Museum. **Los Caracoles** at Escudelleros 14 is a sort of Spanish Hofbräuhaus—huge and always packed.

My favorite restaurants for local-style food are: **Agut** (Calle Gignas 16, huge servings, cheap); **Culleertes** (Calle Quintana 5, a little better); **Siete Puertas** (Paseo Isabel II 14, old and traditional, near the port); the **Casa Isidre** (Calle Flores 12, small, intimate, unknown to tourists); **Florian** (Bertrand y Serra 20, tel. 2124627, higher class); **Casa Jose** (Placa Sant Josep Oriol 10, near Placa Nova, very cheap and popular), and **Jaume de Provença** (Provença 88, tel. 2300029, top place for fish, highest quality, reservations necessary).

GALICIA—THE OTHER SPAIN

Galicia, the northwestern corner of the country, is like a Spanish Scotland. The weather is cooler and often misty, the country-side is hillier and green—and you may even hear Galician bag-pipes droning across the pastures! You're in "Rías" country now, and everything is different.

Rías are estuaries, like drowned valleys, similar to the fjords of Norway but wider and not so steep. Most of them are named after the little towns on their shores, such as Ribadeo, Viveiro, and Cedeira Ferrol.

The Rías Altas, between the river Eo and the Ría of La Coruna, are the most spectacular, with high, steep cliffs, relatively cold water (often with whitecaps), and vast, deserted beaches. The Rías Gallegas, southwest of La Coruna, are not as wild. Almost like lakes with much warmer water are the Rías Bajas (at Corcubión, Muros y Noiya, Arosa, and Pontevedra). These warm beaches are quite popular in July and August.

This corner of Spain may be underdeveloped, but it's one of the oldest places settled by man; the famous cave of Altamira (near Santillana/Santander) is closed to the public due to deterioration of the paintings, but there are excellent reproductions and original artifacts in the little museum nearby. The surprisingly sophisticated cave paintings are 20,000 years old.

The fertile area here was cultivated and influenced by the Celts and Romans. The Celts left us the ruins, the dolmen, and ancient settlements (Citanias). Very impressive Celtic relics can be seen at Monte St. Tekla near Vigo. They also left bagpipes, called Gaita, the national instrument of Galicia. The people are blond and blue-eyed, resembling central Europeans more than "typical" Spaniards.

If you drive through the countryside, you'll see more ox teams pulling carts with massive wooden wheels than modern gasoline-powered equipment. This may be more pastoral and idyllic, but such a paradise has its price: emigration has a long tradition in Galicia. In the villages, you'll find a lot of old people, younger women, and some children. Adult men who can work go to Barcelona, the industrial countries of Europe, or South and North America.

Cocina Gallega

Galician cuisine is a major reason for visiting this area. Treat it as sightseeing for the tongue. It's an indigenous and solid cuisine, and all the ingredients are of the highest quality. In fact, a lot of the seafood served around the Mediterranean coast originates here. Lacón con grelos is the national food of the Gallegos. A little heavy (good for the hard-working people) but excellent, it consists of boiled pork with a sort of green cabbage grown only in Galicia. Along with that, you get potatoes (Europe's best) and chorizo, the spicy smoked sausage. Pote Gallego is a stew prepared from local cabbage, chorizo, bacon, potatoes, beans, and salted pork. Empanadas are flat, round loaves stuffed with onions, tomatoes, bay, and parsley, along with sardines, pork or beef, and sometimes shrimp. Santiago is a good place to find uncountable variations.

For your picnic, try a cheese called La Tetilla and the excellent Galician bread. Both bread and cheese come in the old tried and tested shape (*tetilla* means teat).

Especially along the coast, drop into one of many Marisquerías, or seafood shops, for lobster, shrimp, crabs, mussels, and oysters.

And then there are the excellent local wines. Ribeiro (red and white) is usually served in earthen cups called *cuncas*. Watch the red wine, it's tricky! The white Albarinho, similar to some Portuguese whites, is thought by many to be Spain's best. The best Albarinhos grow in Val de Salnes, north of Pontevedra.

The Galicians like to drink their own wines, so it's not always simple to buy a bottle of these wines—often they are not even bottled but sold only in bars and restaurants. That's just one more reason not to miss supper in one of the many extraordinary Galician restaurants. Don't shy away from the best places. You can eat in Galicia's top restaurants for less than $20.

Transportation

The easiest way to include Galicia in the regular 22-day tour is to travel Madrid-Salamanca-Santiago-Portugal. Take the night train from Madrid (21:40-8:18) or from Salamanca, connecting at Medina del Campo just after midnight. Make Santiago de Compostela your home base in Galicia. Then, from Santiago, hop from town to town south along the Atlantic Coast through northern Portugal to Coimbra.

The cultural landscape of present-day Spain and Portugal was shaped by the various civilizations that conquered the indigenous population and settled on the peninsula. Iberia's warm and sunny weather and fertile soil attracted all early Mediterranean peoples.

The Greeks came to Cádiz around 1100 **B.C.**, followed by the Romans, who occupied the country for almost 1,000 years until **A.D.** 400. The Roman influence remained long after the empire crumbled, including cultural values, materials, and building techniques, even Roman-style farming equipment, which was used well into the nineteenth century. And, of course, wine.

Moors

The Moors—North Africans of the Moslem faith who occupied Spain—had the greatest cultural influence on Spanish and Portuguese history. They arrived on the Rock of Gibraltar in A.D. 711 and moved north. In the incredibly short time of seven years, the Moors completely conquered the peninsula.

They established their power and Moslem culture—but in a subtle way. Non-Moslems were tolerated and often rose to positions of wealth and power. Instead of blindly suppressing the natives by force, the Moors used their superior power and knowledge to develop whatever they found. For example, they even encouraged the growing of wine, although for religious reasons they themselves weren't allowed to drink alcohol.

The Moors ruled for more than 700 years (711-1492). Throughout that time, pockets of Christianity remained. Local Christian kings fought against the Moors whenever they could, whittling away at the Moslem empire, gaining more and more land. The last Moorish stronghold, Granada, fell to the Christians in 1492.

The slow process of the Reconquista (reconquest) resulted in the formation of the two independent states of Portugal and Spain. In 1139, Alfonso Henriques conquered the Moors near present-day Beja in southern Portugal and proclaimed himself king of the area. By 1200, the state of Portugal already had the same borders as today, making it the oldest unchanged state in Europe. The rest of the peninsula was a loosely knit collection of smaller kingdoms until 1469, when Fernando II of Aragon married Isabel of Castilla. Known as the "Catholic Monarchs," they united the other kingdoms under their rule.

The Golden Age

The expulsion of the Moors set the stage for the rise of Portugal and Spain as naval powers and colonial superpowers—the

Golden Age. The Spaniards, fueled by the religious fervor of their Reconquista of the Moslems, were interested in spreading Christianity to the newly discovered New World. Wherever they landed, they tried to Christianize the natives—with the sword, if necessary.

The Portuguese expansion was motivated more by economic concerns. Their excursions overseas were planned, cool, and rational. They colonized the nearby coasts of Africa first, progressing slowly to Asia and South America.

Through exploration (and exploitation) of the colonies, tremendous amounts of gold came into each country. Art and courtly life developed fast in this Golden Age. The aristocracy and the clergy were swimming in money.

The French Baroque architecture that you'll see (like La Granja and the Royal Palace in Madrid) is a reminder that Spain was ruled by the French Bourbon family in the eighteenth century.

Slow Decline

The fast money from the colonies kept them from seeing the dangers at home. Great Britain and the Netherlands also were becoming naval powers, defeating the Spanish Armada in 1588. The Portuguese imported everything, didn't grow their own wheat any more, and neglected their fields.

During the centuries when science and technology in all other European countries developed as never before, Spain and Portugal were occupied with their failed colonial politics.

Endless battles, wars of succession, revolutions, and counter-revolutions weakened the countries. In this chaos, there was no chance to develop democratic forms of life. Dictators in both countries made the rich richer and kept the masses under-privileged.

During World Wars I and II, both countries stayed neutral, uninterested in foreign policy as long as there was quiet in their own states. In the 1930s, Spain suffered a bloody and bitter Civil War between fascist and democratic forces. The fascist dictator Franco prevailed, ruling the country until his death in the 1970s.

Democracy in Spain and Portugal is still young. After an unbloody revolution, Portugal held democratic elections in 1975. Spain, after 41 years of dictatorship, had elections in 1977.

Today, socialists are in power in both countries. They've adopted a policy of balance to save the young democracies and fight problems like unemployment and foreign debts—with moderate success. Spain recently joined the European Economic Community.

ART AND ARCHITECTURE

Art

The "Big Three" in Spanish painting are El Greco, Velázquez and Goya.

El Greco (1541-1614) exemplifies the spiritual fervor of so much Spanish art. The drama, the surreal colors, and the intentionally unnatural distortion have the intensity of a religious vision.

Diego Velázquez (1599-1660) went to the opposite extreme. His masterful court portraits are studies in realism and cool detachment from his subjects.

Goya (1746-1828) matched Velázquez's technique but not his detachment. He let his liberal tendencies shine through in unflattering portraits of royalty and in emotional scenes of abuse of power. He unleashed his inner passions in the eerie nightmarish canvases of his last, "dark," stage.

In this century, **Pablo Picasso** (don't miss his mural, *Guernica*), surrealist **Salvador Dali**, and **Joan Miró** have made their marks.

Architecture

The two most fertile periods of architectural innovation in Spain and Portugal were during the Moorish occupation and in the Golden Age. Otherwise, Spanish architecture follows many of the same trends as the rest of Europe.

The Moors brought Middle Eastern styles with them, such as the horseshoe arch, minarets, and floor plans designed for mosques. Islam forbids the sculpting or painting of human or animal figures ("graven images"), so artists expressed their creativity with elaborate geometric patterns. The ornate stucco of the Alhambra, the striped arches of Córdoba's mosque, and decorative colored tiles are evidence of the Moorish sense of beauty. Mozarabic and Mudejar styles blended Islamic and Christian elements.

As the Christians slowly reconquered the country, they turned their fervor into stone, building churches in both the heavy, fortress-of-God Romanesque style (Santiago de Compostela) and in the lighter, heaven-reaching, stained-glass Gothic style (Barcelona, Toledo, Sevilla). Gothic was an import from France, trickling into conservative Spain long after it swept through Europe.

The money reaped and raped from Spain's colonies in the Golden Age (1500-1650) spurred new construction. Churches and palaces were built using the solid, geometric style of the Italian Renaissance (El Escorial) and the more ornamented Baroque. Ornamentation reached unprecedented heights in

Spain, culminating in the Plateresque style of stonework, so called because it resembles intricate silver filigree work.

In Portugal, the highly ornamented style is called Manueline. The Belem Tower in Lisbon is its best example.

After the Golden Age, innovation in both countries died out, and most buildings from the eighteenth and nineteenth centuries follow predictable European trends.

Spain's major contribution to modern architecture is the Art Nouveau work of Antoni Gaudi early in this century. Many of his "cake-left-out-in-the-rain" buildings, with their asymmetrical designs and sinuous lines, can be found in Barcelona.

History and Art Terms

Alcazaba   Moorish castle.

Alcázar   Initially a Moorish fortified castle, later a residence.

Ayuntamiento   Town hall.

Azulejo   Blue or colored tiles.

Feria   Fair.

Inquisition   Religious and civil courts begun in the Middle Ages for trying heretics and sinners. Punishment ranged from prayer to imprisonment, torture, and death. An estimated 2,000 heretics were burned at the stake during the reign of one notorious Grand Inquisitor.

Moros   Moors. Moslems from North Africa.

Moriscos   Moors converted to Christianity after the victory of the Catholics.

Mozarabs   Christians under Moorish rule.

BULLFIGHTING

The bullfight is as much a ritual as it is a sport, so while no two bullfights are the same, they unfold along a strict pattern.

The ceremony begins punctually with a parade of participants around the ring. Then the trumpet sounds, the "Gate of Fear" opens, and the leading player—el toro—thunders in. An angry half-ton animal is an awesome sight even from the cheap seats.

The fight is divided into three acts. The first is designed to size up the bull and wear him down. The matador, with help from his assistants, attracts the bull with the shake of the cape, then directs him past his body, as close as his bravery allows. After a few passes, the picadors enter mounted on horseback to spear the powerful swollen lump of muscle at the back of the bull's neck. This lowers the bull's head and weakens the thrust of his horns.

In Act II, the matador's assistants (*banderilleros*) continue to enrage and weaken the bull. The unarmed banderillero charges the charging bull and, leaping acrobatically across the bull's path, plunges brightly colored, barbed sticks into the bull's vital neck muscle.

After a short intermission during which the matador may, according to tradition, ask permission to kill the bull and dedicate the kill to someone in the crowd, the final, lethal act begins.

The matador tries to dominate and tire the bull with hypnotic capework. A good pass is when the matador stands completely still while the bull charges past. Then the matador thrusts a sword between the animal's shoulderblades for the kill. A quick kill is not always easy, and the matador may have to make several bloody thrusts before the sword stays in.

Throughout the fight, the crowd shows its approval or impatience. Shouts of *"Olé!"* or *"Torero!"* mean they like what they see—whistling or rhythmic hand clapping greets cowardice and incompetence.

After an exceptional fight, the crowd may wave white handkerchiefs to ask that the matador be awarded the bull's ear or tail. A brave bull, though dead, gets a victory lap from the mule team on his way to the slaughterhouse. Then the trumpet sounds, and a new bull enters to face a fresh matador.

For a closer look at bullfighting, read Hemingway's classic *Death in the Afternoon*.

SPANISH CUISINE

Spaniards eat to live, not vice versa. Their cuisine is hearty food of the people, in big, inexpensive portions.

While not fancy, there is an endless variety of regional special-ties. The two most famous Spanish dishes are paella and gaz-pacho. Paella has a base of saffron-flavored rice as background for whatever the chef wants to mix in—seafood, chicken, pep-pers, and so forth. Gazpacho, an Andalusian specialty, is a chilled soup of tomatoes, bread chunks, and spices. Garlic and olive oil are found to some degree in many Spanish dishes.

The Spanish eating schedule can be frustrating to the visitor. Because most Spaniards work until 19:30, supper (*cena*) is usually served around 21:00, 22:00, or even later. Lunch (*com-ida*) is also served late (13:00-16:00) and is the largest meal of the day. Don't buck this system. No good restaurant will serve meals at American hours.

The only alternative to this late schedule is to eat in tapa bars. Tapas (60 cents) are small portions, like appetizers, of all kinds of foods—seafood, salads, meat-filled pastries, deep-fried tasties, and on and on. You'll find many hungry tourists gulping down dozens of tapas while desperately looking for an open restaurant. Around 21:00 or 22:00, they are totally stuffed and unable to enjoy a great meal in one of the nicely decorated and good restaurants. *Raciónes* are larger portions of tapas—more like a full meal ($2.50). Bocadillos (sandwiches) are very basic. A ham sandwich is just that—ham on bread, period.

The price of a tapa, beer, or coffee is cheapest if you eat or drink standing at the bar or sitting on a bar stool. You may pay a little more to eat sitting at a table and still more for an outdoor table. In the right place, however, a quiet rest over coffee on a floodlit square is well worth any extra charge. The cheapest seats can sometimes give you the best show. Sit at the bar and study your bartender. He's an artist.

Since tapa bars are such a fun part of eating in Spain and have their own lingo as well as a rather strange lineup of food, this list will be a handy tool when hunger beckons:

Tapas

aceitunas olives
albondigas meatballs
almejas clams
anguilas eels
bocadillos sandwiches
boquerones anchovies
cachelos the best potatoes you've ever had (even better in Galicia)

calamares   squid
cebolla   onion
chorizo   red paprika sausage
champiñones   mushrooms
caldo   broth
cocido   stew
ensaladilla Rusia   Russian salad (potato salad)
empanada   fish/meat pastry (pie)—Galicia
fabada   Austrian stew (with white beans)
gamba   Mediterranean shrimp
gazpacho   cold vegetable soup (often served with fried sardines, especially in Andalusia).
guisado   goulash or stew
jamón serrano   special kind of ham. In the bars you can see them hanging from the ceiling.
lacón con grelos   Galician stew
langostinos   giant prawns
lenguado   sole
mariscos   shellfish
pisto   vegetable stew
pulpo   octopus
queso   cheese
queso manchego   sheep cheese of the Mancha
salchichón   salami
salchicha   little sausages
sepia   cuttlefish
sopa   soup
sopa de ajo   garlic soup
sopa de verduras   vegetable soup
ternera   veal
tortilla francesa   omelet, the one you're used to
tortilla Española   potato and onion omelet

Bebidas   When you're thirsty
cerveza (presión)   beer (draft)
sidra   cider
café solo   black espresso coffee
café con leche   coffee with milk
vino tinto/blanco   red/white wine
tinto verano   chilled red wine and lemonade
zumo de naranja   orange juice
agua   water
agua mineral   mineral water
con gas/sin gas   carbonated/without carbonation. (Many visitors start their tour hating the "gas," then gradually fall in love with those tiny bubbles—try it!)
sangría   the dangerous mixture of red wine, sugar, orange juice, lemon juice, brandy, and the kitchen sink.

Postres   Desserts
helado   ice cream
tarta   tart, pie
flan   custard
higos   figs
manzana   apple
leche frita   fried egg/mild pudding

Comidas Cocidas   Cooked meals
While the french-fry maker is the busiest tool in the kitchen of almost every Spanish restaurant, the Spanish language is evidence that there still must exist other ways of preparing food:
asado   roasted
cocido   boiled
tostado   toasted
estofado   stewed
crudo   raw
ahumado   smoked
al horno   baked
a la plancha   grilled on a hot plate
en salsa   in sauce

Desayuno   Breakfast
"Churros and chocolate! I suppose if one searched the restaurants of the world one could not find a worse breakfast nor one that tasted better. The churros were so greasy that I needed three paper napkins per churro, but they tasted better than doughnuts. The chocolate was completely indigestible, but much better than coffee. And the great gobs of unrefined sugar were chewy. Any nation that can eat churros and chocolate for breakfast is not required to demonstrate its courage in other ways."

—James Michener,
Iberia

A typical breakfast consists of coffee or hot chocolate and a roll of some sort. Toast ("'tostada") with butter or churros are the most popular choices.
pan   bread
panecillo   roll
mantequilla   butter
miel   honey
mermelada   marmelade
queso   cheese
embutido   sausage
croissant   croissant
café con leche   coffee with milk

café solo   espresso
huevos revueltos   scrambled eggs
huevos fritos   fried eggs
churros   sugar doughnuts (shaped like cigars)
tostada   toasted roll, with butter or sometimes pâté
chocolate   hot chocolate

Regional Specialties

The dishes of different regions are as varied as you might expect in a country with such deep-rooted regional tendencies.

Galician cuisine has a cult following. Lacón con grelos, boiled pork and cabbage cooked with potatoes and spices, is the indigenous dish. Fresh fish and shellfish, empanadas (meat pies), vegetables and fruit taste just as they should in Galicia.

The French insist that the cuisine gets better as you get closer to the French border. At least it gets a bit fancier. In the north and central high plains, lamb is a good bet. In brash Catalonia, try zarzuela de mariscos (the "operetta of seafood") or their excellent paella.

Moving south, pork out on roast suckling pig in Toledo or Segovia, and try the fried sardines served like french fries in Andalusia. Andalusia is also the home of gazpacho and sangría.

If you can't get to all these regions, Madrid—centrally located and cosmopolitan—is an excellent place for a "cook's tour" sampling of Spain's regional dishes.

Spanish Wine

We think of Spain as only producing cheap, red table wines, and while they do, they also produce perhaps a greater variety of styles than any country. Each region has its own distinct wine.

In general, the north produces the red table wines. Those of Rioja (near the Basque country) are light and oaky and begin to rival the best table wines of France.

Aperitif and dessert wines (sherry, amontillado, fino) are most popular in the hot south, especially Andalusia.

Catalonia produces sparkling wines and brandies, while the central plains prolifically pump out the hearty *vin ordinaire*.

Most large bodegas (wineries) are open for a visit, though it's advisable to phone a few days ahead of time to make arrangements.

PORTUGUESE CUISINE

Portuguese cuisine is different from Spain's but probably not any more different than Andalusian cuisine is from Galician. As in Spain, garlic and olive oil are important in many meals, and seafood is at least as prominent.

An 8 percent service charge is usually included (even if the menu doesn't say so), and a tip is generally not expected. Rounding the bill up, though, is a nice touch.

The Portuguese meal schedule is a bit less cruel, though still unusual for the traveler. Lunch (the big meal) is between noon and 14:00, with supper from 20:00 to 22:00. Perhaps as a result, tapas are not such a big deal. You can eat—and eat well—in restaurants for $5. Here's a list of some specialties you may want to try:

Sopas   Soups
caldo verde   green vegetable soup
canja   chicken broth
sopa alentejana   soup with olive oil, garlic, bread, and eggs
gazpacho   cold, spicy vegetable soup

Peixes   Fish (cheaper than Portuguese meat)
sardinhas assadas   barbecued sardines
linguado   sole
lulas or polvo   octopus
caldeirada   stew of seafood, tomatoes, and potatoes
peixe espada   swordfish
atum   tuna

Mariscos   Shellfish
ameijoas   mussels (try *arroz marisco*)
satola or sapateira   big crab
camaroes   shrimp
gambas   prawn

Carnes   Meat
porco   pork
vitela   veal
vaca   beef
coelho   rabbit
assado   roasted
grelhado   grilled

Bebidas   Drinks
agua   water
bica   cup of espresso
café com leite   white coffee
cerveja   beer
fresco   cold, iced
gelo   ice cream, ice cube
quente   hot
sumo de fruta   fruit juice
vinho tinto   red wine
vinho verde   dry white wine

At a Restaurant
pequeno almoceco   breakfast
almoceco   lunch
conta   the bill
carta   the menu
jantar, ceia   dinner
pimenta/sal   pepper/salt
prato do dia   dish of the day

Portuguese Wine
Portugal is famous for its excellent port wines and dry wines. A refreshing young wine everyone should try is vinho verde. Since much of the best wine is only consumed locally and never really bottled, it's smart to order the always reasonable *vinho da casa* or *vinho de região*.

Branco = white, rosado = rose, tinto = red, seco = dry.

The local aguardente (brandy) is good and cheap. Imported drinks are heavily taxed and very expensive. With such good local varieties, there's really no reason not to drink them exclusively.

Spanish is one of the Romance languages—from Roman Latin—along with Portuguese, French, and Italian. Knowing any one of these helps with some basic Spanish phrases.

Spanish nouns have gender. There are masculine words, generally ending in *o*, and feminine words, ending in *a* or *ion*. The adjectives that describe them must change spelling to match these endings.

Pronunciation

You pronounce Spanish pretty much like it's spelled. Don't "cheat" by slipping into standard American sloppiness. *Peseta* should be "Pay-SAY-tah," not "Puh-SAY-duh."

Spanish is spoken most clearly with the corners of the mouth tight. This should present no problem if you just smile a lot.

Put stress on the next-to-last syllable for words ending in a vowel, *n*, or *s*. Other words are stressed on the last syllable. Exceptions to the rule are marked with an accent (like "Málaga").

Pronunciations vary in different regions of Spain. Don't let it throw you when someone pronounces *cinco*, "THeenko."

Vowels

a   as in f*a*ther
e   almost like the "a" in m*a*ke
i and **y**   as in l*i*ter
o   as in g*o*
u   as in bl*u*e

Consonants

Some letters are different from English pronunciation:
b and **v**   are interchangeable, kind of halfway between b and v
h   silent
j and (soft) **g**   like an h
ñ (with wavy line over it)   like the ni in o*ni*on
r and **rr**   trilled trippingly over the tongue
qu   like k
ll   like the "y" sound in mi*lli*on

Words and Phrases

hello   hola
good-bye   adiós
see you later   hasta luego
goodnight   buenas noches
please   por favor
thank you   gracias

yes/no sí/no
cheap/expensive barato/caro
good/bad bueno/malo
beautiful/ugly bonito/feo
fast/slow rápido/lento
big/small grande/pequeño
very muy
Where is. . .? Dónde está. . .?
How much? Cuánto?
I don't understand. No comprendo.
What do you call this? Cómo se llama ésto?
I'm lost. Me he perdido.
complete price (everything included) todo está incluido
I'm tired. Estoy cansado.
I'm hungry. Tengo hambre.
Cheers! Salud!
food alimento
grocery store tienda de ultramarinos
picnic picnic
delicious delicioso
market mercado
drunk borracho
money dinero
station estación
private accommodations casa particular
toilet retrete, servicio
I yo
you usted
love amor
excuse me perdóneme
You're welcome. De nada.
today hoy
tomorrow mañana
hot caliente
cold frío
with con
and y
but pero
very mucho
all todo
open abierto
closed cerrado
entrance entrada
exit salida
free libre
left izquierda
right derecha

the bill   la cuenta
early   temprano
late   tarde
quickly   rápido
How are you?   Cómo está usted?
Very well, thank you.   Muy bien, gracias.
Do you speak English?   Habla usted inglés?
I don't know.   No sé.
more slowly   más despacio
I am English (or American).   Soy inglés.
Is there a . . . ?   Hay un . . . ?
What?   Qué?
too much   demasiado
Do you have . . . ?   Tiene usted . . . ?
I would like . . .   Gustaria . . .
That's fine.   Está bien.
Monday   lunes
Tuesday   martes
Wednesday   miércoles
Thursday   jueves
Friday   viernes
Saturday   sábado
Sunday   domingo
one   uno
two   dos
three   tres
four   cuatro
five   cinco
six   seis
seven   siete
eight   ocho
nine   nueve
ten   diez
eleven   once
twelve   doce
thirteen   trece
fourteen   catorce
fifteen   quince
sixteen   dieciseis
seventeen   diecisiete
eighteen   dieciocho
nineteen   diecinueve
twenty   veinte
twenty-one   veintiuno
thirty   treinta
thirty-one   treinta y uno
thirty-two   treinta y dos

forty cuarenta
fifty cincuenta
sixty sesenta
seventy setenta
eighty ochenta
ninety noventa
one hundred cien
two hundred doscientos
five hundred quinientos
one thousand mil
six o'clock las seis
half-past six las seis y media
quarter to six las seis menos cuarto
Mr. señor/Sr.
Mrs. señora/Sra.
Miss señorita/Srta.
I have a reservation. Tengo una reserva.
What time? A qué hora?
Have you got a room? Tiene usted una habitación?
bank banco
I would like to change some traveler's checks. Quisiera cambiar unos cheques de viaje.
What is the exchange rate? A cuánto está el cambio?
bus autobús
bus stop parada de autobús
railway station estación
train tren
ticket billete
round-trip de ida y vuelta
first/second class primera/segunda clase
set menu menu del dia
The bill, please. La cuenta, por favor.

SPEAKING PORTUGUESE

Portuguese is like Spanish with a French accent. Unfortunately, even if you know both Spanish and French, it is still difficult to get by in Portugal. Learn a few basic Portuguese words, rely on Spanish (which is widely understood, though not widely spoken), and try hard to pronounce things like the Portuguese.

As in France, the Portuguese use a soft *j* ("zh" sound), soft *ch* ("sh" sound), and speak with a nasal accent. For example, the Portuguese *não* (meaning "no") should sound like "now" said while holding your nose. (Practice this until you *don't* have to hold your nose when ordering in a fancy restaurant.) The Portuguese *s* and the *ç* printed with a little hook or tail are pronounced "sh."

English, French, and especially Spanish are understood by many Portuguese. Though you may not be anywhere near fluent, the Portuguese will appreciate your efforts to speak their language.

Words and Phrases

hello   bom dia   *bawng DEEer*
good-bye   adeus   *erDHEHoosh*
see you later   até logo   *erTAY LOAgoo*
goodnight   boa noite   *BOAer NOYter*
please   por favor   *por faVOAR*
thank you   obrigado   *obree GAHdhoo (women say obree GAHdah)*
yes/no   sim/não   *seeng/nahng*
one/two/three   um/dois/tres   *oong/doysh/traysh*
cheap/expensive   barato/caro   *berRAHtoo/KAHroo*
good/bad   bom/mau   *bawng/mao*
beautiful/ugly   belo/feio   *BEHloo/FAYoo*
big/small   grande/pequeno   *GRAHNder/perKEHnoo*
fast/slow   rápido/lento   *RAHpeedo/LEHNtoo*
very   muito   *MOONGtoo*
Where is . . . ?   Onde está . . . ?   *ONder ishTAH*
How much?   Quanto?   *KWAHNtoo*
I don't understand.   Não compreendo.   *nahng kawngpri-AYNGdoo*
What do you call this?   Como se chama isto?   *KOAmoo ser SHERmer EESHtoo*
I'm lost.   Estou perdido.   *ishTOA perr DHEEdhoo*
complete price (everything included)   tudo incluido   *TOOdhoo engclooEEdhoo*
I'm tired.   Estou cansado.   *ishTOA kern SAHdhoo*
I'm hungry.   Tenho fome.   *TEHnoo FOmer*
Cheers!   Saude!   *serOOdher*

food alimento *alleeMENtu*
grocery store mercearia *merrseaREEab*
picnic piquenique *piknik*
delicious delicioso *debLEEseeozu*
market mercado *merrKAdu*
drunk bebado *beBAdu*
money dinheiro *deeNEERu*
station estacão *eeshtaSAU*
private accommodations casa particular *casa parr-teekuLARR* (or) quartos *kwat roosh*
toilet retrete *rayTRAYtay*
I eu *yo*
you tu *tu*
love amor *amorr*
bank/exchange banco/cambio
I beg your pardon. Desculpe. *deesh kulpuh*
much/little muito/pouco *moien to, poko*
petrol/oil gasolina/óleo
train comboio *kom boy yo*
street/avenue rua/avenida
where onde
when quando
closed fechado
open aberto
beach praia
pensão establishment not quite of the standing of a hotel
pensão residencia room only (no meals available)
pousada state-managed historical hotel
quarto (de casual) bedroom for two persons
quarto com banho room with bathroom attached
marmalade heavy necking session, kissing
peru turkey (the bird)
A tug on your ear lobe means "I like this."

HOURS, SIESTAS, AND FIESTAS

Iberia is a land of strange and frustrating schedules.

Generally, shops are open 9:00 to 13:00 and 15:00 to 19:00, longer in touristy places. Banks are open Monday-Friday from 9:00 to 14:00 (or 13:00, or 13:30), Saturdays from 9:00 to 13:00 and, very occasionally, Monday-Friday 15:30 to 16:30. Restaurants open very late. Museums are generally open from 10:00 to 13:00 and from 15:00 to 19:00. The times listed in this book are for the tourist season. In winter, most museums and sights close an hour early.

There are many regional and surprise holidays. Regular nationwide holidays are:

Portugal—January 1, April 25, May 1, June 10 (national holiday), August 15, October 5, November 1, December 1, December 8, and December 25.

Spain—January 1, January 6, March 19, May 1, June 24, June 29, July 18, July 25, August 15, October 12, November 1, December 8, December 25, Good Friday and Easter, Corpus Christi (early June).

For a complete listing, in English, of upcoming festivals, call or write to the Spanish or Portuguese National Tourist Office (see below).

BASIC INFORMATION

Money

The peseta (pta) is the basic monetary unit of Spain, worth less than a penny in U.S. dollars. In December 1988, there were 150 ptas in US$1.

The Portuguese escudo ($ placed after the number) is approximately the same—120 escudos in US$1.

National Tourist Offices

Some of the best information for planning your trip is just a post-card away. The National Tourist Office of each country is more than happy to send brochures and information on all aspects of travel in their country. The more specific your request (e.g., pousadas, castles, hiking), the better they can help you.

National Tourist Office of Spain: 665 Fifth Ave., New York, NY 10022 (tel. 212/759-8822); 845 N. Michigan Ave., Chicago, IL 60611 (tel. 312/944-0251); and 8383 Wilshire Blvd. #960, Beverly Hills, CA 90211 (tel. 213/658-7188). In Canada: 60 Bloor St. W., Toronto, Ontario (tel. 961-3131).

Portuguese National Tourist Office: 590 Fifth Ave., New York, NY 10036 (tel. 212/354-4403).

Moroccan National Tourist Office: 20 East 46th St., New York, NY 10017 (tel. 212/557-2520); 408 S. Michigan Ave., Chicago, IL 60605 (tel. 312/782-3413); 2 Carlton St., Suite 1803, Toronto, Ontario M5B 1K2 (tel. 416/598-2208).

Telephone Area Codes

Spain 34	**Portugal** 351
Madrid 1	Lisbon 1
Segovia 11	Nazaré 62
Salamanca 23	Obidos 62
Ciudad Rodrigo 23	Évora 66
Sevilla 54	Coimbra 39
Ronda 52	Lagos and Salema 82
Málaga 52	Tavira 81
Granada 58	
Toledo 25	
Barcelona 3	
Santiago 81	

(To dial long distance numbers within Spain, precede each area code with 9.)

Iberian Weather

(1st line, average daily low; 2nd line, ave. daily high; 3rd line, days of no rain)

	J	F	M	A	M	J	J	A	S	O	N	D
Spain												
Madrid	33	35	40	44	50	57	62	62	56	48	40	33
	47	51	57	64	71	80	87	86	77	66	54	48
	22	19	20	21	22	24	28	29	24	23	20	22
Barcelona	42	44	47	51	57	63	69	69	65	58	50	44
	56	57	61	64	71	77	81	82	67	61	62	57
	26	21	24	22	23	25	27	26	23	23	23	25
Málaga	47	48	51	55	60	66	70	72	68	61	53	48
	61	62	64	69	74	80	84	85	81	74	67	62
	25	22	23	25	28	29	31	30	28	27	22	25
Portugal												
Lagos/ Algarve	47	57	50	52	56	60	64	65	62	58	52	48
	61	61	63	67	73	77	83	84	80	73	66	62
	22	19	20	24	27	29	31	31	28	26	22	22
Lisbon	46	47	49	52	56	60	64	65	62	58	52	48
	56	58	61	64	69	75	79	80	76	69	62	57
	22	20	21	23	25	28	30	30	26	24	20	21

BACK DOOR CATALOG

ALL ITEMS FIELD TESTED, HIGHLY RECOMMENDED,
COMPLETELY GUARANTEED AND DISCOUNTED BELOW RETAIL.

The Back Door Suitcase/Rucksack $60.00

At 9"x21"x13" this specially designed, sturdy functional bag is maximum carry-on-the-plane size (fits under the seat). Made of rugged waterproof Cordura nylon, with hide-away shoulder straps, waist belt (for use as a rucksack), top and side handles, and a detachable shoulder strap (for toting as a suitcase). Lockable perimeter zippers allow easy access to the roomy (2200 cu. in.) central compartment. Two outside pockets are perfect for books and other frequently used items. Over 8,000 Back Door travelers have used these bags around the world. Rick lives out of one for 3 months at a time. Comparable bags cost much more. Available in navy blue, black, grey, or burgundy.

Moneybelt $6.00

Required! Ultra-light, sturdy, under-the-pants, nylon pouch just big enough to carry the essentials comfortably. I'll never travel without one and I hope you won't either. Beige, nylon zipper, one size fits all, with instructions.

Catalog . . . . Free

For a complete listing of all the books, products and services Rick Steves and Europe Through the Back Door offer you, ask us for a copy of our 32-page catalog. It's free.

Eurailpasses

With each Eurailpass order we offer a free taped trip consultation. Send a check for the cost of the pass you want along with your legal name, a proposed itinerary and a list of questions and within two weeks we'll send you your pass, a taped evaluation of your plans, and all the train schedules and planning maps you'll need. Because of this unique service, we sell more train passes than anyone on the West Coast.

Back Door Tours

We encourage independent travel, but for those who want a tour in the Back Door style, we do offer a 22-day "Best of Europe" tour. For complete details, write to us at the address below.

All orders will be processed within one week and include a one year's subscription to our Back Door Travel newsletter. Add $1.00 postage and handling to each order. Washington state residents add 7.8% sales tax. Sorry, no credit cards. Send checks to:

Europe Through the Back Door
120 Fourth Ave. N. • Edmonds, WA 98020 • (206) 771-8303

22 Days Series: Travel Itinerary Planners
These pocket-size guides are a refreshing departure from ordinary guidebooks. Each author has in-depth knowledge of the region covered and offers 22 carefully tested daily itineraries. Included are not only "must see" attractions but also little-known villages and hidden "jewels" as well as valuable general information. 128 to 144 pp., $7.95 each
22 Days in Alaska by Pamela Lanier (28-68-0)
22 Days in the American Southwest by Richard Harris (28-88-5)
22 Days in Asia by Roger Rapoport and Burl Willes (65-17-3)
22 Days in Australia by John Gottberg (65-03-3)
22 Days in California by Roger Rapoport (28-93-1)
22 Days in China by Gaylon Duke and Zenia Victor (28-72-9)
22 Days in Europe by Rick Steves (65-05-X)
22 Days in France by Rick Steves (65-07-6)
22 Days in Germany, Austria & Switzerland by Rick Steves (65-02-5)
22 Days in Great Britain by Rick Steves (28-67-2)
22 Days in Hawaii by Arnold Schuchter (28-92-3)
22 Days in India by Anurag Mathur (28-87-7)
22 Days in Japan by David Old (28-73-7)
22 Days in Mexico by Steve Rogers and Tina Rosa (65-04-1)
22 Days in New England by Anne E. Wright (28-96-6)
22 Days in New Zealand by Arnold Schuchter (28-86-9)
22 Days in Norway, Denmark & Sweden by Rick Steves (28-83-4)
22 Days in the Pacific Northwest by Richard Harris (28-97-4)
22 Days in Spain & Portugal by Rick Steves (65-06-8)
22 Days in the West Indies by Cyndy and Sam Morreale (28-74-5)

"Kidding Around" Travel Guides for Children
Written for kids eight years of age and older. Generously illustrated in two colors with imaginative characters and images. Each guide is an adventure to read and a treasure to keep.
Kidding Around San Francisco, Rosemary Zibart (65-23-8) 64 pp., $9.95
Kidding Around Washington, D.C., Anne Pedersen (65-25-4) 64 pp., $9.95
Kidding Around London, Sarah Lovett (65-24-6) 64 pp., $9.95

All-Suite Hotel Guide: The Definitive Directory, Pamela Lanier
Pamela Lanier, author of The Complete Guide to Bed & Breakfasts, Inns & Guesthouses, now provides the discerning traveler with a listing of over 600 all-suite hotels. (65-08-4) 285 pp., $13.95

Asia Through the Back Door, Rick Steves and John Gottberg
Provides information and advice you won't find elsewhere—including how to overcome culture shock, bargain in marketplaces, observe Buddhist temple etiquette, and even how to eat noodles with chopsticks! (28-58-3) 336 pp., $11.95

Buddhist America: Centers, Practices, Retreats, Don Morreale
The only comprehensive directory of Buddhist centers, this guide includes first-person narratives of individuals' retreat experiences. (28-94-X) 312 pp., $12.95

Bus Touring: Charter Vacations, U.S.A., Stuart Warren with Douglas Bloch
For many people, bus touring is the ideal, relaxed, and comfortable way to see America. Covers every aspect of bus touring to help passengers get the most pleasure for their money. (28-95-8) 200 pp., $9.95

Catholic America: Self-Renewal Centers and Retreats, Patricia Christian-Meyers
Complete directory of over 500 self-renewal centers and retreats in the United States and Canada. (65-20-3) 325 pp., $13.95

Complete Guide to Bed & Breakfasts, Inns & Guesthouses in the United States and Canada, 1989-90 Edition, Pamela Lanier
Newly revised and the most complete directory available, with over 5,000 listings in all 50 states, 10 Canadian provinces, Puerto Rico, and the U.S. Virgin Islands. (65-09-2) 520 pp., $14.95

Elegant Small Hotels: A Connoisseur's Guide, Pamela Lanier
This lodging guide for discriminating travelers describes hotels characterized by exquisite rooms and suites and personal service par excellence. (65-10-6) 230 pp., $14.95

Europe 101: History & Art for the Traveler, Rick Steves and Gene Openshaw
The first and only jaunty history and art book for travelers makes castles, palaces, and museums come alive. (28-78-8) 372 pp., $12.95

Europe Through the Back Door, Rick Steves
For people who want to enjoy Europe more and spend less money doing it. In this revised edition, Steves shares more of his well-respected insights. (28-84-2) 404 pp., $12.95
Doubleday and Literary Guild Book Club Selection.

Gypsying After 40: A Guide to Adventure and Self-Discovery, Bob Harris
Retirees Bob and Megan Harris offer a witty and informative guide to the "gypsying" life-style that has enriched their lives and can enrich yours. Their message is: "Anyone can do it!" (28-71-0) 312 pp., $12.95

The Heart of Jerusalem, Arlynn Nellhaus
Arlynn Nellhaus draws on her vast experience in and knowledge of Jerusalem to give travelers a rare inside view and practical guide to the Golden City. (28-79-6) 312 pp., $12.95

Mona Winks: Self-Guided Tours of Europe's Top Museums, Rick Steves and Gene Openshaw
Here's a guide that will save you time, shoe leather, and tired muscles. It is designed for people who want to get the most out of visiting the great museums of Europe. (28-85-0) 450 pp., $14.95

The On and Off the Road Cookbook, Carl Franz and Lorena Havens
A multitude of delicious alternatives to the usual campsite meals. (28-27-3) 272 pp., $8.50

The People's Guide to Mexico, Carl Franz
This classic guide shows the traveler how to handle just about any situation that might arise while in Mexico.
"The best 360-degree coverage of traveling and short-term living in Mexico that's going." — *Whole Earth Epilog* (28-99-0) 587 pp., $14.95

The People's Guide to RV Camping in Mexico, Carl Franz and Lorena Havens
This revised guide focuses on the special pleasures and challenges of RV travel in Mexico. Includes a complete campground directory. (28-91-5) 304 pp., $13.95

The Shopper's Guide to Mexico, Steve Rogers and Tina Rosa
The only comprehensive handbook for shopping in Mexico, this guide ferrets out little-known towns where the finest handicrafts are made and offers tips on shopping techniques. (28-90-7) 200 pp., $9.95

Traveler's Guide to Asian Culture, Kevin Chambers
An accurate and enjoyable guide to the history and culture of this diverse continent. (65-14-9) 356 pp., $13.95

Traveler's Guide to Healing Centers and Retreats in North America, Martine Rudee and Jonathan Blease
Over 300 listings offer a wide range of healing centers—from traditional to new age. (65-15-7) 224 pp., $11.95

Undiscovered Islands of the Caribbean, Burl Willes
For the past decade, Burl Willes has been tracking down remote Caribbean getaways. Here he offers complete information on 32 islands. (28-80-X) 220 pp., $12.95

Automotive Repair Manuals
Each JMP automotive manual gives clear step-by-step instructions together with illustrations that show exactly how each system in the vehicle comes apart and goes back together. They tell everything a novice or experienced mechanic needs to know to perform periodic maintenance, tune-ups, troubleshooting, and repair of the brake, fuel and emission control, electrical, cooling, clutch, transmission, driveline, steering and suspension systems and even rebuild the engine.
How to Keep Your VW Alive (65-12-2) 410 pp., $17.95
How to Keep Your Golf/Jetta/Rabbit Alive (65-21-1) 420 pp., $17.95
How to Keep Your Honda Car Alive (28-55-9) 272 pp., $17.95
How to Keep Your Subaru Alive (65-11-4) 420 pp., $17.95
How to Keep Your Toyota Pick-Up Alive (28-89-3) 400 pp., $17.95
How to Keep Your Datsun/Nissan Alive (28-65-6) 544 pp., $17.95
How to Keep Your Honda ATC Alive (28-45-1) 236 pp., $14.95

Other Automotive Books

The Greaseless Guide to Car Care Confidence: Take the Terror out of Talking to Your Mechanic, Mary Jackson
Teaches the reader about all of the basic systems of an automobile. (65-19-X) 200 pp., $14.95

Off-Road Emergency Repair & Survival, James Ristow
Glove compartment guide to troubleshooting, temporary repair, and survival. (65-26-2) 150 pp., $9.95

Road & Track's Used Car Classics, edited by Peter Bohr
Features over 70 makes and models of enthusiast cars built between 1953 and 1979. (28-69-9) 272 pp., $12.95

Ordering Information

Fill in the order blank. Be sure to add up all of the subtotals at the bottom of the order form and give us the address whither your order is to be whisked.

Postage & Handling

Your books will be sent to you via UPS (for U.S. destinations), and you will receive them in approximately 10 days from the time that we receive your order. Include $2.75 for the first item ordered and $.50 for each additional item to cover shipping and handling costs. UPS shipments to post office boxes take longer to arrive; if possible, please give us a street address.

For airmail within the U.S., enclose $4.00 per book for shipping and handling.

All foreign orders will be shipped surface rate. Please enclose $3.00 for the first item and $1.00 for each additional item. Please inquire for airmail rates.

Method of Payment

Your order may be paid by check, money order, or credit card. We cannot be responsible for cash sent through the mail.

All payments must be made in U.S. dollars drawn on a U.S. bank. Canadian postal money orders in U.S. dollars are also acceptable.

For VISA, MasterCard, or American Express orders, use the order form or call (505)982-4078. Books ordered on American Express cards can be shipped only to the billing address of the cardholder. Sorry, no C.O.D.'s. Residents of sunny New Mexico, add 5.625% tax to the total.

Back Orders

We will back order all forthcoming and out-of-stock tit¹es unless otherwise requested.

All prices subject to change without notice.

Address all orders and inquiries to: **John Muir Publications**
P.O. Box 613
Santa Fe, NM 87504   **(505)982-4078**

ITEM NO.			TITLE	EACH	QUAN.	TOTAL
		.				
		.				
		.				
		.				
		.				

Postage & handling (see ordering information)* _____

New Mexicans please add 5.625% tax _____

Total Amount Due _____

Credit Card Number: _____

Expiration Date: _____ Daytime telephone _____

Name _____

Address _____

City _____ State _____ Zip _____

Signature X _____

Required for Credit Card Purchases